EAST LONDON

Edited by Donna Samworth

First published in Great Britain in 2003 by
YOUNG WRITERS
Remus House,
Coltsfoot Drive,
Peterborough, PE2 9JX
Telephone (01733) 890066

All Rights Reserved

Copyright Contributors 2003

HB ISBN 1 84460 128 5
SB ISBN 1 84460 129 3

FOREWORD

Young Writers was established in 1991 as a foundation for promoting the reading and writing of poetry amongst children and young adults. Today it continues this quest and proceeds to nurture and guide the writing talents of today's youth.

From this year's competition Young Writers is proud to present a showcase of the best poetic talent from across the UK. Each hand-picked poem has been carefully chosen from over 66,000 'Hullabaloo!' entries to be published in this, our eleventh primary school series.

This year in particular we have been wholeheartedly impressed with the quality of entries received. The thought, effort, imagination and hard work put into each poem impressed us all and once again the task of editing was a difficult but enjoyable experience.

We hope you are as pleased as we are with the final selection and that you and your family will continue to be entertained with *Hullabaloo! East London* for many years to come.

CONTENTS

Ivy Owusu-Ansah	1

Baden Powell Primary School

Jamaine Renzulli	1
Zahid Iqbal	2
Donovan Samuels	2
Genevieve Wynter	3
Lee Campbell	4
Zainab Vankad	4
Zerin Erdogan	5
Jordan Cole	6
Terrie Gemal	6
Mikayla Healy	7
Rasheedah Lynch	7
Remel Talor	8
Rianne Hibbert	8
Rui Gollop	9
Shakara Joseph	10
Berivan Dugunyurdu	10
Ryan Alleyne-Rowe	11
Osekhodion Alli	12
Shakilah Barry	12
Chanelle Clarke-Bridet	13
Ryan Auguste	13
Bianca Willer-Smith	14
Hydar Munthakim	14
Shalby Scarlett	15
Robert Carnie	16
Sophia Loren	16
Tequila Taylor	17
Samad Munthakin	17
Leanna Anderson	18
Shanice Webb	18
Victoria Ault	19
Ayo Osunsami	19

	Adeshola Fujah	20
	Danny Spurling	20
	Jaz Daley	21
	Grace Sofuyi	21
	Carlena Shanetel Clarke	22
	Asilhan Demirci	22
	Jayce Ault	23
	Ramone Reid	23
	Ayobami Sanusi	24
	Callum Quidley	25
	Jade Graham	25
	Shane Davis	26
	Sukwinder Singh	26
	Haydn Samuels	27
	Daniel Passam	27
Canonbury Primary School		
	James Dessurne	28
Chase Lane Junior School		
	Spencer Goldberg	28
	Jason Plumb	29
	Hannah Solinunte	29
	Kelly Tucker	30
	Saeed Piperdi	30
Edinburgh Primary School		
	Byran Malcolm	31
	Suleman Khokhar	31
	Naomi Hinds	32
	Dawood Yousuf	32
	Sana Khan	33
	Nazia Khan	33
	Aneesa Shakoor	34
	Brook-lynn Lewis	34
	Nosheen Ahmed	35
	Sonia Miah	35
	Emily Rimmer	35

Gainsborough Primary School
- Jemay Abdullah — 36
- Sandra Wilson — 36
- Shuchita Kabir — 37
- Bonita Kabir — 38
- Freddie Sparks & Tommy Love — 38
- Princess Hebden — 39
- Farzana Kobir — 39
- Funmi Ajayi — 40
- Lizzie Njuguna — 40
- Jermaine Izukanne — 41
- Samuella Nyarko — 41
- Olaolu Oyawoye — 42
- Emma Larter — 42
- Ramone Hanson-Mathurin — 43
- Amaury Pacheco — 43
- Salih Nulucan — 44
- Lauren Rickwood — 44

Gatehouse School
- Maisie Robinson — 45
- Priyesh Patel — 45
- Fanny-Lee Franklin — 46
- Kyneil Grant — 46
- Harry Maynard — 47
- Hannah Muldoon — 48
- Antonia Miller — 48
- Amy Porter — 49
- Mai Ann Le — 50
- Toni McGinley — 50
- Harriet Lewis — 51
- Abisoye Osundairo — 52
- Elder Sencer — 52
- Georgina Maynard — 53
- Joshua Charles — 54
- Olivia Cole — 54
- Oliver Albert — 55
- Oscar Langmead — 55

Tamara Ishida	56
Ryan Mitchell	56
Katie Glover	57
Lauren Newman	57
Jack Kirby	58
Omar Rashid	58
Vanessa Albert	59
Marie Deenmamode	59
Andrew Isaias	60
Andrew Moodley	60
George Hanness	60

Guardian Angels RC JM & I School

Rosie Inns	61
Nicole Campbell	61
Ebisiemen Ajayi	62
Themba Green	62

Gwyn Jones Primary School

Adam Mansoor	63
Alice Claussen	64
Indiana Richard	65
Christopher Waddington	65
Laura Waller	66
Jaylan Konrad-Lee	66
Shannon Maher	67
Uwais Qasmi	68
Shireen Loonat	68
Amber Wilks	69
Zeke Bruney	69
Matthew Harvey	70
Thomas Keirle	70
Emma Tye	71
Rebecca Boot	71

Handsworth Primary School

Ella O'Donnell	72
Georgina Hurlock	72

Alice Butcher	73
Jahmel Perkins	74
Caroline Harvey	74
Yasmin Cromwell	75
Abbie Lunn	76
Pavan Chamdal	76
Anna Panayi	77
Annie Hutchinson	78
Alexander Baker	78
Sian Barrett	79
Oliver Barker	79
Samuel Smith	80
Michael Carroll	80

Larkswood Junior School

Somar Ibrahim	81
Lana Heath	81
Vanessa Regresado	82
Reade Mulvany	83
Thomas Purver	84
Esme Humphries-King	84
Jacqueline Kilikita	85
Nicola Morris	85
Harry Kane	86
Charlie Clayton	86
Tom Frater	87
Regan Fielder	88
Fiona Hynds	88
Samuel Verdin	89
Jason Maduro	90
Georgie Yianni	90
George Powell	91
Kane Slisz	91
Billie Poppy	92
Mitchell House	92
Katie Goodland	93
Jonathan Palmer	93
Nikki Drewett	94

Sam Hollis	94
Charis Thoma	95

Longshaw Primary School

Monique Ventour	95
Amber Zakrzewski	96
Jack Button	96
Philippa McAnulty	97
Francesca Astin Herrera	97
Callum Kousoulou	98
Anna-Maria Katsimigos	99
Natalie Mills	100
Amy Barnes	100
Lauren Cadogan	101
Zoe Scicluna	101
Sonia Soomessur	102
Abbie Loman	102
Richard Brown	103
Emily Nichols	103
Rojdan Gul	104
Shanice Attram	104
Yasmin Halil	105
Anoushka Russell	105
Rippley Gallagher	105
Bonnie Wingfield	106
Stephanie Karagiannidis	106
Jade Nash	107
Prima Patel	107
Sasha Robinson-King	107
Stephanie Smith	108

Monega Primary School

Uroosa Malik	108
Hazara Khatun	109
Rohoney Ravi	109
Iftikhar Ahmed	110
Nazish Mahmood	110
Shahhan Spall	111

Kemi Quadri	112
Shahina Rahman	112
Thasnima Begum	113
Sajna Mitha Choudhury	114
Judita Jasiunaite	114
Husnain Nasim	115
Amina Gull	115
Kayrul Mirza	116

St Joseph's Convent School, Wanstead

Molly Kerrigan	116
Farah Omotosho	117
Sophia Plent	117
Porshia Athow	118
Chantal Purser	118
Harriet Rose Halsey	119
Claudia Zeppetella	120
Tessa Kerslake	120
Ayesha Nicholls	121
Alicia Hempsted	122
Louise Lasfer	122
Jessica Moruzzi	123
Georgia Briggs	124
Olivia Andani	124
Faith Robins	125
Niamh Sheehy	126
Pascale Bourquin	127
Tumi Unuefa	128
Harriet Blackshaw	128
Sophie Radford	129
Sarah Hart	129
Elizabeth Delima	130
Rachel Bonsu	130
Jasyme Robinson-Martin	131
Martha Wilkinson	132
Olivia Smart	132
Akua Owusu-Ansah	133
Georgia Downes	133

Louise Cottle	134
Christine Stokes	135
Nicola Johnson	136
Clare Davis	136
Isabelle Innes-Taylor	137
Jessica Lebon	137
Charlotte Crawford	138
Katherine Dadswell	139
Thanupriya Sureshkumar	140
Hannah Sullivan	141
Louisa Grieve	141

Salisbury Primary School

Catherine Oyinlola	142
Rebecca Lewis	142
Musleh Uddin	143
Albulena Meha	144
Kulshan Bhakar	144
Isheetah Islam	145
Terri Gibbs	146
Masum Hussain	146
Aderinsola Dada	147
Samantha Hampton	147
Sheun Oshinbolu	148
Bilal Anwar	148
Candice Terrelonge	149
Edirin Idogun	149

Selwyn Primary School

Fawzan Ismail	150
Fatima Patel	150
Daniel Drakes	151
Lukman Hasan	152
Chhaya Mistry	152
Leena Gunamal	153
Manisha Gunamal	154
Raheema Azam	155
Robinah Kironde	156

Seven Mills Primary School
- James Parmenter — 156
- Jamie Murch — 157
- Maria Luu — 157
- Sharmila Haque — 158
- Shahina Begum — 158
- Tasnia Foyaze — 159
- Harry Davidson — 159
- Ella Scrutton — 160
- Mitchel Skeels — 160
- Flaheen Alam — 161
- Ikramul Hoque — 161
- Louis Sleap — 162
- Jodie Cox — 162
- Nahid Hoque — 162
- Nima Begum — 163

Shapla Primary School
- Marjana Chowdhury — 163
- Abidur Rahman — 164
- Farheen Begum — 164
- Najmen Akhter — 165
- Azizul Haque — 166
- Shrmin Shanaz — 166
- Nasir Uddin — 167
- Nayem Ahmed — 168
- Faroqul Islam — 168
- Mizan Rahman — 169
- Shubey Begum — 169
- Farhana Begum — 170
- Sayeem Yaheya — 170
- Farhana Lucky Rouf — 171
- Junel Ali — 171
- Abdul Azim — 172
- Amena Ahmed — 172
- Masuda Hoque — 173
- Samad Hussain — 173
- Shamina Begum — 174

Farzana Begum	174
Mujibul Hoque Miah	175
Shourov Ahmed	175
Tawhid Choudry	176
Sayma Begum	176
Nazia Begum	177
Hafsa Rahman	177
Fatema Begum	178
Shahid Mohammad	178
Muntaha Wadud	179
Ataur Rahman	179
Amrina Jahan	180
Ibrahim Khalil	180
Abul Khaled	181
Jalal Uddin	181
Irina Sulltana Jahin	182
Farhana Kadir	183
Mohammed Ashraf Hussain Chowdhury	183
Iqbal Hussain	184
Aminul Islam	184

Snaresbrook Primary School

Gemma Beswick	185
Yasmeen Mukadam	185
Archanna Gunasekaram	186
Lydia Clark	186
Sehar Ishaq Khan	187
Matthew William Hill	188
Shauna Jane Butler	188
Harriet Clarke	188
Pippa Wiskin	189
Alexander McKie	189
William Brown	190
Rebecca Adams	190

Wanstead Church Primary School

Alice Roe & Rhys Jones	191
Imogen Steinberg	191

Ellen Phillipson	192
Elise Woolnough	192
Rosie-May Mary Parker	193
Justin Hung & Carys Jones	193
Ellen Hepworth	194
James Hall & Nadine Baker	194
Priscilla Hampton	195
Rebecca Fanning	195
Caitriona Elizabeth Ferguson	196
Christopher Gardner	196
Chloe Buck	197
Madeleine Greene	197
Grace Tierney	198
Grace Twinn	198
Daniel Mannion	199
Joe Rees	199
Amy Iona Fanning	200
Aimee Evans	200
Madeleine Simpson	201
Anna McGetrick	201
Charlotte Springett	202
Christopher Churchett	202
Melissa Relfe	202
Heather Yarwood	203
Nicholas Allen	203
Georgia Surridge	203
Bethany Walker	204
Paul Andrew Gardner	204
Katie Alice McLean	204
Joshua Owusu-Afriyie	205
Freddie Cocker	205
Zoe Aves	205
Charlotte Hall-Munn	206
Erin Cobby & John Hagon-Torkington	206

Whittingham Primary School

George Tollady	206
Rachael Clouter	207

Keian Brissett-Martin	207
Yewande Oloruntade	208
Emillie Hill	208
Saniya Ahsan	209
Naomi Benjamin	210
Yousr Tabir	210
Andrew Christou	211
Zara Marie Ahsan	212
Michael New	212
Gamal James	213
Arnold Kaloki	214
Hansah Shafiq	214
Alex Du-Gal	215
Rebecca Scott	215
Zuharia Arshad	216
Jordene Battye	216
Dionne Cottoy-Rogers	217
Leah Martin	217
Millie Carter-Phillips	218

The Poems

SILENT SINGER

The silent singer would only stay,
for just one hour but not a day.

He would come to the gardens to
sing and sing, but when sunrise came
he went out with a ping.

He looks so waxy on the outside,
but you just give him a chance don't go and hide.

For the clothes he wears may not suit you
but can you guess who is who?

For the silent singer would only come
in the dark night.

But is never seen in the morning
light . . .

Ivy Owusu-Ansah (11)

SNOW

Snow, snow, hard and soft.
Snow, snow, smooth and rough.
Snow, snow, white and cold.
Snow, snow, moves quickly and hits.
Snow, snow, fair and fast.
Snow, snow, is a group, is a club.
Snow, snow, bold and fat.

Jamaine Renzulli (9)
Baden Powell Primary School

SWIMMING

Swimming is my favourite
Swimming is fun
Swimming is cool
And swimming is for everyone.
Swimming is happiness
Swimming is not bad
You will learn swimming
So don't feel bad.

Swimming is great
Swimming is nice
Swimming is good
So come, swim
Along with me.

Swimming is warm
Swimming is cheerful
Swimming is exciting
And swimming is joyful.
Swimming has a big pool
Swimming is nice
Swimming is good
For you and me.

Zahid Iqbal (9)
Baden Powell Primary School

THE SNOW

The snow is low,
And people go, 'Ho, ho!'
The wind blows like thunderstorms,
The lands are white and trees are bare,
Full of snow, it looks like underwear.
People ride in sleighs and ski on hills.

People row through icy storms,
And play snowfights
With snowballs.
People are wrapped in coats and scarves,
People in houses and beds.

Donovan Samuels (8)
Baden Powell Primary School

MY AUNTIE MARY

My auntie Mary is a right fairy
She can be quite contrary.

She can be clean rather than mean
Although she hasn't been seen.

She's just been so clean that she always
Washes her jeans.

Whenever
She comes
To stay
I always have
To play with
Her and she
Always takes all
Day that's why
She always has
To pay me in May £30
Ha, ha, ha!
Mad innit?

Genevieve Wynter (10)
Baden Powell Primary School

LEE'S ROOM AND AUNTIE MARY

My room it's hullabaloo
The green and blue
Relaxing room.
So weirdly shaped
It's so untidy
You just don't want to leave.
It's like me
Generous.
When I am down
It's there for me,
Then the worst happens.
My auntie Mary comes.
My auntie Mary
Is a right hairy beast
Who is quite contrary.
She can be rather mean than clean.
She can be a drama queen
In her dressing gown
And can be a clown,
Always has a frown
Makes a lot of sound,
A lot of people get wound up by her.
She always does acrobatics
On the ground.
My mum comes in and I pop.

Lee Campbell (11)
Baden Powell Primary School

THE MAGIC WAND

I have a magic wand from my mother
When I use it, it's nice and bendy
In my room I keep it nice and covered
When it's broken I easily mend it.

I use it in shows
I always use it.
I have it when I want milk from cows
I never lose it.

Zainab Vankad (7)
Baden Powell Primary School

MY AUNTIE JEAN, YOU KNOW WHAT I MEAN

I'd sooner be
Dumped and pumped and thumped
Than get kissed by my auntie Jean
You know what I mean.

I'd sooner be
Hugged and mugged and jugged
Than get kissed by my auntie Jean
You know what I mean.

Whenever
she
comes
to
stay
she
gives
me
a
whacking
smacking
kiss.
    Yuck!

Zerin Erdogan (11)
Baden Powell Primary School

SNOW

Snow is so cold
Snowballs are fun
That's why I like snow
But when it turns into ice
It's as much fun
You can't make snowballs or snowmen
Your mummy always says, 'Don't run'
Especially if you're playing football or other sports.
I like making a snowman
Then I take a little bit of snow
Then throw it at them and they won't try to get me.
I'll keep on doing it to them
Then no one will be able
To get me, maybe
One person!

Jordan Cole (9)
Baden Powell Primary School

SILENCE, SILENCE EVERYWHERE

Silence, silence everywhere.
Why is there silence
Everywhere?
At home! At school!
Silence, silence is
All around me.
Silence, silence
Everywhere.

Terrie Gemal (8)
Baden Powell Primary School

Portrait Of A Mermaid

If I were an artist
I'd paint a
portrait of a mermaid.

To do a proper job
I'd take all the
colours from the world.

First I'd paint the tail
pink like a
fat snake.

Second I would paint
the eyes blue
like the ocean
and the sky.

Mikayla Healy (9)
Baden Powell Primary School

Winter In November

November in a spinner
spinning in the mist,
weaving such a lovely web
with gold and amethyst.
In among the shadows dark
in the night please don't say,
'Don't let the bed bugs bite!'
Because if they do
just get your shoe
and beat them till they're black and blue.

Rasheedah Lynch (8)
Baden Powell Primary School

HACKNEY MAN

My name is McSweety,
I come from Hackney
All the girls like me
They think I'm funny
That's how I get all the money in Hackney.

If you wanna see me just come to me
If you wanna see me just come to my party
If you wanna see me, see McSweety.

I've gotta mummy and a daddy
They're so lovely.
They give me some kiss, kiss,
With a hiss, hiss.
They give me some money
To buy my airforce ories.

If you wanna see me just come to me
If you wanna see me just come to my party.
If you wanna see me, see McSweety.

Remel Talor (9)
Baden Powell Primary School

MY MUM

My mum is a pineapple,
My mum is an apple,
My mum is a sweet,
My mum is kind,
My mum is sweet,
My mum is a plum,

My mum is an orange,
My mum is a wonderful ring,
My mum is a party girl,
My mum is nice and kind,
My mum loves singing songs,
My mum is my mum and that's that.

Rianne Hibbert (9)
Baden Powell Primary School

THE SUN, WIND AND RAIN

The wind, in all shapes and sizes,
The wind, nibbling at your ears
Like squirrels eating chestnuts.
The wind carrying noises in one ear
and out the other.
The wind, pushing you back and pushing you forward.

The sun, round and sizzling,
The sun, changing your colour.
The sun, heating you up
like twigs near a fire.
The sun, giving you light
when you most need it.

The rain, cold and wet,
The rain, grey and miserable.
The rain, dropping on you like
bullets from the sky.

Rui Gollop (11)
Baden Powell Primary School

My House

My house is *sooo* big
I feel *sooo* small
Sometimes I crawl on the floor
And then someone knocks at my great big door.

My room is full of so much stuff
But sometimes it just makes me want to huff.

I walk in my front room
And then I pick up the spiky big broom
I throw it around but it doesn't make any sound.

My mum walks in
I begin to tidy up
She throws the cup.

I run and hide
I feel so small
Sooo small
Sooo small
Sooo small.

Shakara Joseph (11)
Baden Powell Primary School

My Mum

My mum is the best
My mum is kind
My mum loves us.
We love our mum
My mum is bright
My mum is pretty

My mum is clear
My mum is clever
My mum is cheerful
My mum enjoys everything
My mum is smooth
My mum is safe.

Berivan Dugunyurdu (9)
Baden Powell Primary School

MY PORTRAIT OF A UNICORN

If I were an artist
I'd paint the portrait
of a unicorn.

For his head I'd use a
3D cardboard and paint
it white.

For his body I'd shape a
3D board and decorate it
with glitter.

For his hooves I will
find four shiny magnets.

For his tail I will shave
someone bald and use
their hair.

And for his horn I will
get a giant drill.

Ryan Alleyne-Rowe (10)
Baden Powell Primary School

HOW CHRISTMAS DAY COMES

How December comes,
Slowly by slowly,
How December comes.
On Christmas Day it is lovely,
People come to other people's houses.
People come and cook food
And they all eat in the house of joy
And happiness.
How they sing beautifully in different countries,
Like Mexico, Nigeria, they have some good Christmas Days.
How it comes on 26th
If it's someone's birthday
And how wonderful it is.
How wonderful!

Osekhodion Alli (9)
Baden Powell Primary School

THE SNOWMAN

The snow is white
The snow is falling
The snow is lovely and white.
We can play snow fights.
The snow is smooth
We can make a snowman.
The snow is lovely, white and peaceful.

Shakilah Barry (8)
Baden Powell Primary School

SNOW

Cold snow I love so much,
It will freeze you hard if you touch.
Snow, snow, when it drops from the sky,
It goes so fast that you can't see it pass.
Snow, you see it everywhere, on the ground,
A snowball made of snow.
Children making gigantic snowballs,
Then adding it to the snowman to make him tall.
Snow, you see it fall to the ground,
Now I will tell my friend how snow I have found.
Snow, it is my friend,
And will be to the very end.
Now you know how I love snow!

Chanelle Clarke-Bridet (8)
Baden Powell Primary School

THE SNOW

The snow is white,
The snow can make snowmen,
The snow can make the wind cold,
The snow covers everything.
The snow can make a blizzard,
The snow can kill leaves,
The snow is beautiful
The snow comes from Russia.
The snow can pour on Christmas Day
The snow is lovely.

Ryan Auguste (8)
Baden Powell Primary School

A Portrait Of A Mermaid

If I were an artist
I'd paint a portrait
of a mermaid.

To do a proper job
I'd use colours from
the world.

First I would start on her long, curly
golden hair like the shell on a snail.

Next I'd do her round face shaped
like a round clock.

For her blue eyes I'd paint them as
blue as the ocean.

Last I'd paint the rest of her face and
stomach and her green scales on her back like
the scales on a green snake.

Bianca Willer-Smith (10)
Baden Powell Primary School

Never Mind

Never mind if you're hot,
Never mind if you're cold.
Never mind if you're quiet,
Never mind if you're loud.
Never mind if you're tall,
Never mind if you're short.
Never mind if you're fat,
Never mind if you're slim.

Never mind if you're bored,
Never mind if you're happy.
Never mind if you're slow,
Never mind if you're fast.
Never mind if you're quiet,
Never mind if you're loud,
Because you'll be the same.

Hydar Munthakim (8)
Baden Powell Primary School

TEN THINGS ABOUT SHELLS

You can bend it
lend it, always send
it up to the sky
which is so so high.

We can hear it, stare at it,
always can be near to it.

They can use it as a boat
see how it floats!
Beat it like a drum.

Some shells can be
the shape of my thumb.

Spell it out loud and be very proud.

S - h - e - double L
If you pat it on the back
I wouldn't turn black.

Shalby Scarlett (9)
Baden Powell Primary School

My Friend The Shoelace Twiddler

He's my friend the shoelace twiddler,
the shoelace diddler.
He's the class fiddler.
People go, look at that diddler
and I go, he's my friend the shoelace twiddler.

When it's time to get up from our seats and go out to play,
He gets up and falls over because in class he's fiddled
and twiddled and tied his shoelaces together
so he falls over.
People go, look at that fiddler
and I go, he's my friend the shoelace twiddler.

He's the shoelace twiddler,
The shoelace diddler.
The world's greatest shoelace fiddler.

Robert Carnie (11)
Baden Powell Primary School

Portrait Of A Unicorn

For his head I'd use a white pillow,
For his body I'd have a white cushion's wool.
For hooves I'd borrow white paint
For his tail I'd use a white silver star,
And for his horn I'd need pure white snow.

If I were an artist I'd paint the portrait of a unicorn,
To do a proper job and I will
Borrow colour from the world.

Sophia Loren (10)
Baden Powell Primary School

Portrait Of A Unicorn

If I were an artist
I'd paint the portrait
Of a unicorn.

To do a proper job
I'd borrow colours
From the world.

For his head I'd use a white snow.
For his body I'd have a unicorn rolling in the snow.
For his hooves I'd borrow crystal golden hooves.
For his tail I'd use a little white pillow.
For his horn I'd use glittery gold.

Tequila Taylor (9)
Baden Powell Primary School

Portrait Of A Unicorn

If I were an artist I'd paint a portrait of a unicorn
I'd use colours from the world.
I'd use a white snowflake from the sky, falling down.
For his body I'd have blue and white from the sky.
For his hooves I'd borrow brown from the mud.
For his tail I'd borrow black from outer space.
I would also need a silver and gold sword.
He is a unicorn of wind, he lives in the sky.

Samad Munthakin (10)
Baden Powell Primary School

MY MUM AND DAD

My mum and dad are cool
Hippy-hip cool
They're the best like all the rest
I love them so hippy-hip much.

My brother is rude
My dad is cool
My mum is the best like all the rest.

My dad raps to my mum
And my mum raps to my dad
My brother raps to the west
Like all the rest.

So that's all from my mum and dad
and brother for now.

Leanna Anderson (8)
Baden Powell Primary School

A SHARPENER

It can sharpen a carrot
If you had three you can make steps
for a mouse.

Fifty can make a house
You can take out the blade to cut
Cheese or bread.

If you were a mouse you can shave your
legs or chin.
If you were drawing you can draw around it.

You can smash it on the floor, but you can't eat it.

Shanice Webb (10)
Baden Powell Primary School

MY LIFE

When I wake up in the morning,
I stretch.
Then I get in the bath,
But I suddenly laugh.
After I get my clothes on,
I eat my breakfast.
I brush my teeth,
Then I go to school.
School is OK (sometimes),
Most of the time it is boring.
Most of the time I am snoring.
When I get home I am glad to be home
And I feel like I don't want to go back.
I play on my PlayStation 2 for a minute,
Then I go to bed and that is the end of that.

Victoria Ault (10)
Baden Powell Primary School

THE HULLABALOO PARTY

I'm going to a party called Hullabaloo!
You better make sure you're bringing
Chocolate or pancakes too.
It's a scary party with Scooby Dooby, Doo.
This is an echoing room, a room
Full of food, a room with balloons.
Hullabaloo, this is red and blue
With loads of kids and adults too.
Hullabaloo.

Ayo Osunsami (10)
Baden Powell Primary School

A PORTRAIT OF PHOENIX

If I were an artist I'd paint a portrait of a
Phoenix.

To do a proper job I'll borrow colours
from the world.

For its head I'll need every primary colour
because it's colourful.

For its hair I'll need a flame because its hair
is bright orange.

For its tidings I'll borrow a rainbow of bright
as can be from the sky.

For its legs I'll use a stick
the most brightest one in the world.

Adeshola Fujah (9)
Baden Powell Primary School

TEN THINGS TO DO WITH A TENNIS BALL

You can roll it on the floor,
You can throw it at a door.

You can bounce it up and down,
You can spin it round and round.

You can give it to a dog,
You can lose it in the fog.

You can dump it in a garden
You can also make it harden.

You can smack it in a tree,
Sorry, got to go because I threw it to Lee.

Danny Spurling (9)
Baden Powell Primary School

HULLABALOO SPORTS

Michael Jordan slam dunks,
the crowd go wilder than a stampede
of elephants.

Robert Pires scored for Arsenal
the crowd was so loud you could hear them
from the Eiffel Tower.

Tiger Woods pots a ball in the hole.
The crowd goes so crazy that they hit each
other with clubs.

Tim Henman whacked the ball over the stadium,
the crowd rushed at him with tennis balls.

        Why do crowds go wild?

Jaz Daley (10)
Baden Powell Primary School

WHAT IF...

What if the flower wasn't red?
What if the sky wasn't blue?
What if people were not there?
What if people were orange?
What if school was closed?
What if I was an egg?
What if people were always upset?
What if there wasn't light?
What if there wasn't any dictionaries?
    What if?
        What if?
            What if?

Grace Sofuyi (9)
Baden Powell Primary School

MY PORTRAIT OF A MERMAID

If I were an artist
I'd paint the portrait
of a mermaid.

To do a proper job
I'd borrow colours
from the world.

For her hair I'd use a range of gold and yellow
from the Queen's palace
For her fins I'd use a range of green grass in a field.
For her necklace I'd use some pearls from a jewellery shop.
For her hair band I would make it out of flowers from sea anemones.
For her eyes I'd borrow some children's marbles.
For her skin I'd use some soft white snow.

Carlena Shanetel Clarke (10)
Baden Powell Primary School

SNOW

Snow is nice because it is snow,
Snow is nice because it is slow,
Snow is cold and colder and the coldest
Because it's snow.
Snow is slow, snow coldest and snow,
Snow melts when it's sunny because it is sun,
The sun melts snow because it is shiny, shinier and
shiniest because it is the sun,
Snow, snow where are you?
I can see myself but not you,
Snow, snow I can see you on cars but not on me,
The trees cried for you just for you, snow, snow.

Asilhan Demirci (8)
Baden Powell Primary School

PORTRAIT OF A UNICORN

If I was an artist
I would paint the portrait of a unicorn
I'd use colours from the world.

For his head I'd use a
cloud from a sunny valley.

For his body I'd use a
mist from the bottom of a waterfall.

For his hooves I'd use painted
clay from the world.

For his tail I'd use
thousands of black strings from a mighty black goat.

For his horn I'd use a tusk from a great elephant.

Jayce Ault (9)
Baden Powell Primary School

TEN THINGS TO DO WITH A BASKET

You could shape something like a cake
You can use it to carry food.

You could use it as a hat
You can use it to carry water.

You can use it to put pencils in
You can use it as a fake hat with drawing on.

You could use it as a pot with a short handle.
You can carry jewellery in it.

Ramone Reid (10)
Baden Powell Primary School

PORTRAIT OF A UNICORN

If I were an artist
I'd paint a portrait
Of a unicorn.

To do a proper job
I'd borrow colours
From the world.

For his head
I'd use a shade of
Silvery white cloud.

For his body
I'd have a creamy white
Paint from the walls of Rome.

For his hooves
I'd borrow lead from a freshly
sharpened pencil.

For his tail
I'd use the white from
a pebble washed in from a tide.

And for his horn
I'd need an ice cream cone that
had gone hard.

Ayobami Sanusi (10)
Baden Powell Primary School

PORTRAIT OF A UNICORN

I'd use a thick, white
paint for his head.

I'd use a big,
white cloth for
its body.

I'd borrow black,
shiny, small shoes.

I'd use a long,
black wig for
his tail.

I'd need a carrot
but spray it silver
for his horn.

Callum Quidley (10)
Baden Powell Primary School

UNICORN

If I was an artist I would paint a picture of a unicorn.
For his head I'd use a snowy white crystal.
For his body I'd have a shiny white body.
For his hooves I'd borrow black tyres.
For his tail I'd use a shiny material.
For his horn I'd need a blue crystal.

Jade Graham (10)
Baden Powell Primary School

WHAT YOU CAN DO WITH A DARNING MUSHROOM

Use it to mush food or
use it as a spinning top.
Pretend it is a mushroom
and put it in a garden.
You can use it as a screw
for a giant wooden horse
and use it for a hammer
if you didn't have one.
You can use it as an
umbrella if you were really small!

These are just a few ideas
but there must be one hundred more.

Shane Davis (10)
Baden Powell Primary School

A PORTRAIT OF A UNICORN

If I were an artist I'd paint a
portrait of a unicorn.
To do a proper job I'd borrow a mixture
of paint colours.
For his head I'd use a white cloud like a statue.
For his body I'd have white, silvery, glittery clothing.
For his hooves I'd borrow a baby's little shoes.

For his tail I'd use a black fake hair.
And for his horn I'd need a big, pointy, sharp,
silver magic wand.

Sukwinder Singh (9)
Baden Powell Primary School

MAGICAL STYLE

Nobody can see my style on me
It is always inside of me.

My style is on me
But for some reason
Nobody can see my style on me.

That's why
I always say
Magical style is on me.

Do you know what I mean
It's a magical dream.

Haydn Samuels (11)
Baden Powell Primary School

FEELINGS

I want to feel the breeze waving on my arm,
I want to feel the skin of a slithering snake,
I want to feel a tiger looking for prey,
I want to capture the feeling of a monkey flowing through a tree.
I want to feel a bat swooping through the sky.

Daniel Passam (8)
Baden Powell Primary School

BEING ABLE TO FLY

My little mouse flies around the house,
We both went up the tree,
he flew with me.

When I fly,
I don't want to die,
I love my wings,
that my mouse always brings.

My mouse loves to fly,
but he never cries,
the mouse gets chased by the cat
and tries to get under a hat.

I also see birds
in herds.
The mouse likes his sausages
but the boy likes porridges.

The mouse always runs under the mat,
but the cat is always too fat.

When the mouse always runs under the mat,
the boy can't catch the cat.

When the mouse runs near the toaster
the boy can never write a poster.

James Dessurne (7)
Canonbury Primary School

MY BABY BROTHER

My baby brother is so dumb,
All he does is suck his thumb.
He always goes round his friend Maisy's,
When all she says is whoopsy daisy.

When he plays hide-and-seek,
He cheats and always peeks.
My baby brother is so dumb
All he does is suck his thumb.

Spencer Goldberg (7)
Chase Lane Junior School

PEACE

Wars are bad,
They make us sad.
We fear forever,
Living our lives in terror.
Treat each other like a friend,
Then wars should hopefully come to an end.

Jason Plumb (11)
Chase Lane Junior School

TEACHERS

Teachers teach you all you need to know.
Sunshine, rain or even snow.

Doing all the marking, books up on their knee.
Sitting in the staffroom drinking cups of tea.
Maths is numbers, division, too.
English is writing, there's so much to do.

Hannah Solinunte (8)
Chase Lane Junior School

OUR TEACHER LOST HIS VOICE TODAY!

It happened to be Monday morning,
The children had arrived as the day was dawning.
Then suddenly appeared our teacher,
Who seemed to have an unusual feature.

Then all of a sudden the silence broke,
As he came out with an awful croak.
And then Andrew Wread-Heart piped up,
'I think he's lost his voice!'

So kids everywhere looking under tables, chairs
And inside books,
Until he started to give us those looks,
Finally John Thomas said,
'You can have my voice instead!'

Kelly Tucker (10)
Chase Lane Junior School

MY LOVELY HOME

I have a lovely home,
With every single thing,
A mother and a father,
And a front doorbell to ring.
A dining room and a kitchen,
Some bedrooms and a hall,
But the baby brother in the cradle,
Is the nicest thing of all.

Saeed Piperdi (11)
Chase Lane Junior School

ANGER AND HAPPINESS

Anger is a rain cloud shot by a dark black arrow.
Anger tastes like melting lava on my tongue.
Anger smells like a mountain full of burning rubber.
Anger looks like a man-eating, bloodsucking alien tracking plant.
Anger sounds like nails scratching on a blackboard.
Anger feels like my heart is tearing apart.

Happiness is a yellow sunshine.
Happiness tastes like sweet ice cream.
Happiness looks like a floating lily pad.
Happiness smells like amazing air freshener.
Happiness sounds like the early birds singing.
Happiness feels like a bear's fur.

Byran Malcolm (10)
Edinburgh Primary School

FEAR

Fear is the dark angel of death waiting to strike.
It is like Hell burning with red-hot fire.
The smell is like burnt ashes.
It looks like a dark black shadow ball
surrounding Earth making it pitch-black.
It feels like you're locked in a dark room.
Fear is always with you and will never go away.
The dark angel of death is waiting for the right moment
of your painful death.

Suleman Khokhar (10)
Edinburgh Primary School

WHY'D YOU DO IT?

Why'd you do it Grannie dear?
Why'd you push him off the pier?
Why'd you drive him round the bend?
Why'd you put his life at end?

Why'd you do it Grampa dearest?
Why'd you shoot the first and nearest?
Why didn't you just capture it?
Why don't you pull off feathers bit by bit?

Why'd you do it Mumsie dear?
Why'd you cut off his whole ear?
Why'd you do it to Daddie too?
Why'd you do it, Dad how are you?

Why'd you do it Daddie dearest?
Why'd you stab the far and nearest?
Why'd you stab an alligator?
Are you not the terminator?

Why'd you do it family?
Why'd you give me pain not glee?
Why, Mummie, Daddie, you're hurting me?
Why you are mad, I can't see.

Naomi Hinds (10)
Edinburgh Primary School

LEAVES

My flaming colour leaves are playing together
Zooming up the oak tree
towards the flaming old sun
like the two legendary birds
so beautiful
laughing like the Japanese legend says.

Dawood Yousuf (10)
Edinburgh Primary School

WHY NOT STOP?

Bullying starts with racism!
Always ends up with criticism!
Why do it? There's always a reason!
If you don't stop you'll end up in prison!
Is that how you've been treated, or is that what you've been taught?
What if you end up in prison, what if you get caught?
Because of all you bullies
Nobody lives life in ease, nobody is ever in peace!
There is no *love*, there is no *colour*!
The brightness disappears!
The smiles on our faces
Turn to buckets of tears!
Why be insane
And drive yourself down the wrong lane?
You'll end up in *double trouble!*
Why punch and kill people with a chain?
You're not being clever, you're being insane!
You might mash their brain!
And end up yourself in bare pain!
Why make a pitch-black stain in your heart?
Hurry up you've got time, make a new start!

Sana Khan (11)
Edinburgh Primary School

SADNESS

Sadness is dull grey,
It tastes like sour lemon.
Sadness smells like burnt toast.
It looks like tears dripping down cheeks.
Sadness sounds like someone screaming for help.
It feels like a heart is broken.

Nazia Khan (11)
Edinburgh Primary School

MY FAVOURITE DAY

The snow was pleasant and silky silvery snow
The tall trees were dark green but they changed to
proper white like cotton wool.

We made a snowman
It was sparkling like stars in the sky.
It was shimmering like sea in the sunlight.
The snow covered everything
Wow!
It was so exciting and enjoyable!

Aneesa Shakoor (10)
Edinburgh Primary School

THE LITTLE SAUSAGE

I have a little sausage that speaks
another language and I
received it in a package.

It has one eye and a tiny tie which looks
so funny I want to die.

The sausage has been with me for a year
then one day it disappeared
but I didn't even cry a tear.

Brook-lynn Lewis (11)
Edinburgh Primary School

MY LAVA LEAF

My lava leaf zoomed off the tree like a rocket,
It's lighter than a bucket,
It's pointy as a knife.
My lava leaf plunged off the tree like a rocket
falling on the ground, but it was yet alive.
My lava leaf's colour is red and orange like the flaming sun.
Its shape is like a French bun.

Nosheen Ahmed (10)
Edinburgh Primary School

HATRED!

Hatred is a fierce black.
It tastes like nothing just plain.
Hatred smells like a hot lava.
It looks like big red eyes gleaming at me.
It sounds like a branch creaking.
It feels like my heart is beating.

Sonia Miah (10)
Edinburgh Primary School

HAPPINESS

Happiness is jazzy orange colouring the world
Happiness tastes like creamy strawberry ice cream
melting in my mouth.
Happiness smells like red roses swaying in the wind.
Happiness looks like a golden river meandering up to Heaven.
Happiness sounds like a hummingbird singing softly.
Happiness feels like the touch of velvet running through my fingers.

Emily Rimmer (11)
Edinburgh Primary School

ANIMAL TEACHERS

Miss Wally
Can sometimes be a big bully.

Miss Bryan
Can roar like a lion.

Mr Simpson
Can shout so you better watch out.

Miss Ryan
Can steam like an iron.

Mr Pete
Can smell like feet.

Mr Jay
Knows the way.

Mr Bat
Wears a nice hat.

Mr Tree
Hums like a bee.

Mr Rabbit
Has a bad habit.

Jemay Abdullah (10)
Gainsborough Primary School

THE HORSE

Funny neigh, swaying mane
Dazzling galloper, loves the rain
Sugar eater, water drinker
With two loving winkers.

Steel shoes, bringer of news,
Beautiful fur, smells like myrrh
Girl's toy, hates naughty boys
Good company, named Bethany.

Sandra Wilson (10)
Gainsborough Primary School

THE FLOWER

Dead and sleepy,
Lifeless and still.
Dozing away
On top of a hill.

Petals droop down
Touching the ground.
Everything dreaming
All around.

Suddenly one day
The sun peeps out
Then out from the ground
Comes a little sprout.

Swaying its leaves,
From side to side
Finding a little place
To hide.

Shuchita Kabir (11)
Gainsborough Primary School

MY FIRST DATE!

I love this boy in my school;
Although he sometimes acts like a fool
Today it is Valentines,
So I asked him for a date,
I hope he doesn't come too late.

He never knew about Cupid
He might like him because he's stupid.
He is like an angel,
Looking at me straight in the eyes,
I hope when I marry him, he doesn't tell lies.

He always gives a fright,
With his glittering glimmering sight.
What would his mother say?
I hope I'm not a pain,
And it's all not in vain.

Bonita Kabir (9)
Gainsborough Primary School

THE SAD MAN

I was sitting on a roof feeling a bit sad
When I realised things were not that bad
I had a vision of me being poor
Then I saw myself walking through a door
Through the door I saw a man
Then I realised he was holding a can
I looked in the can and saw lots of money
Then in a flash I saw lots of honey.

Freddie Sparks (11) & Tommy Love (10)
Gainsborough Primary School

THE LONELY DESERT

The desert is so silent,
It has an open space,
It's so wide
I can have a fast race.

There's a beautiful river nearby,
But it's just about to die,
It is so weak,
I can see a bird's beak,
It has been filled with so many rocks,
And none went in my socks.

The desert is so hot,
I have to get a pot,
It has been destroyed by aliens out of space!

Princess Hebden (8)
Gainsborough Primary School

THE LOUD STORM ATTACK

The thunder's too loud!
Move it out!
Help me pour it all about!

The thunder's too loud!
I can hear it from the clouds!
I wish I never said anything about it now.

Farzana Kobir (11)
Gainsborough Primary School

CHRISTMAS IS JUST ROUND THE CORNER

Christmas is soon, lots of things to do
Wrap the presents . . . I don't know what to get for little Lou.

Xbox consoles for the boys,
Barbie dolls and some other toys.

Just wait until the children see the presents
I am not sure if they will like it, I find it pleasant.

I've come back from the shops
Oh no, forgot the turkey in the parking lot.

Not to worry most of the neighbours are vegetarians
. . . and I thought cooking it would make me a humanitarian.

The kids keep pestering me what to get
I'm thinking about getting them a cat for a pet.

Funmi Ajayi (10)
Gainsborough Primary School

THE MAGNIFICENT COBRA

My cobra is green like a frog jumping to attack,
His eyes are like grey shining pebbles.
His nose is like a dog's nose, wet and always running.
His scales are like a bright star in the night.
He resembles the summertime because he always has a smile
                                                            on his face.
I will make you my friend and you will be my king and
                                          I will be your queen.

Lizzie Njuguna (9)
Gainsborough Primary School

THE DESERT IS SO HOT

The desert is so hot the way the sun burns,
It's a big place where I can run with lots of pace,
I need some water, I see some ahead,
I walk so far I'll need a bed.

The desert is so lonely I see anyone,
A camel with a man comes, I ask him for a ride,
Then behind comes the pride,
I ask him again for a ride, he says yes happily.

We get to a place full of sand more than I've ever seen,
I see something made of sand,
I see some boys playing like a band.

Jermaine Izukanne (8)
Gainsborough Primary School

THE STORM

The storm is as hungry as a lion,
with its sharp yellow claws,
it pounces up upon you
with its scary, frightening paws.

The storm is a monster,
who has no friends
It cries like a baby,
in its shifty and scary bends.

Samuella Nyarko (10)
Gainsborough Primary School

LOVE POEM

My love is like a gentle touch,
My heart is in the air,
I love you like I love my rose,
And I always know you care.

My soul is always on hold,
To wait for your love to come,
My soul is always cold,
Without you I can't love anyone.

It is Valentine's Day today,
Please come to me always,
But when it is May,
I know you'll come to say I love you.

Olaolu Oyawoye (8)
Gainsborough Primary School

MY BROTHER - KENNING

Milk-drinker,
Bad-thinker,
Potty-hater,
Toy-taker,
Nappy-lover,
Cosy-cover,
Marshmallow-eater,
Loves his sister,
Cheeky-giggler,
That's my brother.

Emma Larter (11)
Gainsborough Primary School

TREE - KENNING

A tree is a . . .
Paper-maker
Food-giver
Seed-dispersal
Reproducer
Shelter-giver
Dog-hater
Air-giver
Leaf-dropper
Hug-giver
Autumn-hater
It's a tree!

Ramone Hanson-Mathurin (10)
Gainsborough Primary School

MY DOG - KENNING

Cat-chaser,
Meat-eater,
Face-licker,
Best-runner,
Ribena-drinker,
Smart-thinker,
Born-licker.

Amaury Pacheco (11)
Gainsborough Primary School

MY DOG - KENNING

My dog,
Noise-maker,
Mess-giver,
Home-watcher,
Park-lover,
Lover-giver,
Bone-crusher,
Hole-digger,
My dog.

Salih Nulucan (10)
Gainsborough Primary School

I'M LAUGHING

I'm laughing mad!
    Funny! Happy!
I'm laughing ridiculously
    Loud!
I'm laughing tremendously!
    Crazy! Hysterically! Hilariously!
I'm laughing loudly! Screaming!
I'm laughing mad!

Lauren Rickwood (9)
Gainsborough Primary School

RIDDLE POEM

I eat carrots
I'm much bigger than parrots.

My name is Marrel
My belly's as big as a barrel.

I give a kick
I also lick.

I am quite wide
I give a ride.

When you kick
You make me quick.

You don't have much luck
When I buck.

I do not fly
Who am I?

Maisie Robinson (8)
Gatehouse School

MY ANIMAL POEM

Dogs are nice
And so are mice.
Birds are loud
And lions are proud.
Badgers are shy
Foxes are sly.
Tigers are stripey,
Their names are Mikey.

Priyesh Patel (10)
Gatehouse School

DAY OUT AT THE ZOO

Once I went to the zoo
And when I saw the caged animals, I went, *'Boo hoo.'*
'How sad is this?' I cried out loud,
'It cannot be allowed.'

I saw a tiger standing proud,
And when he roared it came out loud.
His colours were orange and black.
I got bored so I turned my back.

The giraffe was tall.
Soon there was a crowd, zoo keepers and all.
His neck was long,
I loved the way he ran along.

The penguins were very small,
They weren't exactly tall.
Their colours were black and white,
They didn't give me a fright.

Fanny-Lee Franklin (8)
Gatehouse School

RIDDLE POEM

I feed on flies
Sometimes I die
My legs are thin
I hide in the bin.

They think I'm nasty
I'm very dusty.
Who will buy me?
Will it be you?

I feed on everything
Sometimes I die.
My legs are short
And people step on me.

They like me
Because I'm tickly.
I'm small
Who am I?

Kyneil Grant (8)
Gatehouse School

MOONY, THE MOON DEVIL CAT

Moony is a cat of many,
At day he is God's son,
But when he leaves the heavens
He goes down, far down to the underworld
To take the Devil's throne.
So beware, do not be fooled,
Do not fall under his spell
For when the moon shines
The cat will turn into the feline mastermind.

So with his power and brains
He will conquer every bit of the plains.
But he only has so long
Before the moon wanes
Then he will be nothing but a
Pussycat again.

Harry Maynard (8)
Gatehouse School

THE THINGS OF MISTER NOBODY THERE

The things of Mister Nobody there
They dance and prance and they do it in the air.

I am the shoes of Mister Nobody there
I danced on the table, I danced on the chair
And while I danced my heels kept the beat
I am the shoes that move without feet.

The things of Mister Nobody there
They dance and prance and they do it in the air.

We are the cards of Mister Nobody there
We play by ourselves and we play in a pair
And we shuffle ourselves
As we lay on the shelves.

The things of Mister Nobody there
They dance and prance and they do it in the air.

Hannah Muldoon (11)
Gatehouse School

GUESS WHO I AM

I'm a bit like a beaver and like a duck,
To guess who I am you'll need some luck.
I'm the size of a rabbit,
And have more than one bad habit.
I'm one of three mammals who lays eggs,
And I have four very short legs.
Who am I?

I have enough poison to kill a small dog,
I live underwater so I don't need to worry about fog.
I have fur,
And a spur.
No shoes will fit on my feet,
And I never get a name like Philip or Pete.
Who am I?

Antonia Miller (9)
Gatehouse School

I HEARD...

I heard a raindrop fall from the sky,
I heard a scream coming from outside.
I heard footsteps pounding upstairs,
I heard a door creaking open.
I heard the trees whistle into the sky,
I heard a chair collapse onto the floor.

I heard a cat crawling up the stairs
I heard a cat miaow through the walls.
I heard a clock ticking from downstairs,
I heard a clock strike twelve.
I heard a cat purring so loud,
I heard her rush for a bird.

I heard a bird scream so loud,
I heard the cat leap onto the bird,
I heard her rip and tear the bird,
I heard her crunch and tear the bird.
I heard her burp so loud with joy,
I heard her run back inside.

Amy Porter (10)
Gatehouse School

HURRIEDLY

Hurriedly I changed at dawn
Hurriedly I dressed to keep warm
Hurriedly I packed my case
Hurriedly we went on the airport chase
Hurriedly we ran in the rain
Hurriedly we boarded the plane
Hurriedly the pilot landed at last
Hurriedly through customs we passed
Hurriedly we booked a hotel wearily
Hurriedly my mum whistled merrily
Hurriedly I ran down to the beach
Hurriedly I saw Brooke eating a peach
Hurriedly I ran and kicked her leg
Hurriedly she cried to Meg
Hurriedly I unpacked my case
Hurriedly I walked to pace
Hurriedly I went to sleep
Hurriedly I had a dream to keep
Hurry is a blizzard but most hurried of all
Is my best friend's dad who has a hurry call.

Mai Ann Le (10)
Gatehouse School

DANCE

Be free with emotion
Let the music take over
Let it take over with elation
Don't ever let it stop.

Let the rhythm go through you
Let it go through your veins
Let it flow to your imagination
Express it with dance.

Melody has to catch you
Inspire you to do what your heart desires
The dance goes in and out of you
In an instant.

Toni McGinley (11)
Gatehouse School

WHAT IS IT?

The dog asked
His friend and
His friend asked
The cat.
Who was that
At the door?
The cat told
The dog's friend
And he told
The dog
That it was the gardener.
But the dog was
Clever enough to know
That he came on Thursdays.
He told his friend
Who went to ask the cat again.
The cat laughed
And said it was
The boy next door.
So the dog's friend nodded
And went to tell the dog.

Harriet Lewis (10)
Gatehouse School

I Thought I Heard...

I thought I heard a ladybird sing a song,
I thought I heard a kangaroo moo,
I thought I heard a horse groan,
I thought I heard a rabbit say, 'Thank you,'
I thought I heard a fish sing a melody,
I thought I heard a butterfly snort.

I thought I heard a bumblebee chirp,
I thought I heard a cat bark,
I thought I heard a piglet squeak,
I thought I heard a ship purr,
I thought I heard a piglet quack,
I thought I heard a rock scream.

I thought I heard a dog say, 'Ahoy,'
I thought I heard a deer say, 'To be or not to be,'
I thought I heard a cat say, 'Atomic kitten,'
I thought I heard a lion burp,
I thought I heard an elephant trumpet so loud,
I thought I heard a chicken cry.

Abisoye Osundairo (10)
Gatehouse School

The Sea

The sea is full of beauty and colour,
The seabed is like a jungle,
The waves of the sea run like horses in the ocean,
In the morning the sea is calm and still.

The Lord of the sea is greedy.
All the precious jewels lie buried in the deep.
In these crystals lies a curse,
The curse of the under sea.

Treasure seekers beware!
He who reaches down too far
Will be forever cursed.
Bad luck will follow him to the grave.

There lies an anchor
The ship beside it wrecked.
The pirates paid the price for good
All that is left of them, their bones.

Elder Sencer (10)
Gatehouse School

I FELT...

I felt an oak twined with leaves,
I felt the waves ripple my feet,
I felt the sand cling to my skin,
I felt a feather brush my face,
I felt a flower span my fingers,
I felt the clouds float by.

I felt the moon fall down with strength,
I felt the sun rise its head,
I felt the raindrops patter down,
I felt the wind whack my face,
I felt the snowflakes glide in the sky,
I felt the hail descend from above.

I felt the tears of heavenly joy,
I felt the gloom of sorrow,
I felt the despair of loneliness,
I felt spite of angriness,
I felt the elation of success,
I felt gratitude for my earnings.

Georgina Maynard (10)
Gatehouse School

DEEP BLUE

The light reflecting on the calm sea waves
But under the waves is a whole different land.

This land has no sky
Only a ceiling of silent waves
And at the bottom a shipwreck stands.

Priceless jewels and treasure alike,
All these precious things can never be touched.
For a curse lies upon them
The curse of the deep blue sea.

No man has lived the awful curse
The curse of the deep blue sea.

Joshua Charles (11)
Gatehouse School

HURRIEDLY

Hurriedly I ran down the stairs
Hurriedly I ate a pear
Hurriedly I went to school
Hurriedly I fell in the pool
Hurriedly I got pulled out
Hurriedly I was left in doubt
Hurriedly we drove back to school
Hurriedly I had my food
Hurriedly I went off home
Hurriedly I watched a programme on Rome
Hurry is the word that teachers use
But most of all is the daily news.

Olivia Cole (10)
Gatehouse School

WILD CAT

In the daytime he's quiet and dreamy.
In the night he's vicious and screamy.

He's nice and cuddly in the day
But at night he scares me, takes my breath away.

His claws are sharp to tear out flesh
To eat it raw and eat it fresh.

But when he's cuddly, he's really nice
He never uses weapons such as a knife.

Oliver Albert (9)
Gatehouse School

ANIMALS

Cheetahs are fast
Elephants are last
Monkeys are daft,
They have a bath
While hyenas laugh.
Foxes are sly,
Cats never die.
Leopards look like lightning
Tigers are frightening.
Cats have claws,
While a lion roars.

Oscar Langmead (10)
Gatehouse School

THE TOMCAT

In the night he gives a fright,
The cat that I have now.
He scratches at the door and cries a loud miaow.

In the day he is tame and happy,
The cat that I have now.
He wails for his milk and cries a quiet miaow.
He sleeps in the bedroom,
He sleeps on the floor,
He rests in the bathroom,
He wails at the door.

But in the night he is a vicious feline
That wails to the moon.

He might be an alley cat,
He might be something else,
But he is a fierce feline.

Tamara Ishida (8)
Gatehouse School

MY SNAKE

My snake is quick as a lightning bolt,
His colour's red,
Yellow
And orange.
His teeth are like little sharp pins with a deadly snap,
When he is calm and at rest,
He is as still as a stick on the forest floor.

Ryan Mitchell (10)
Gatehouse School

WINTER

Winter is near
Time for cheer
With a bottle of beer.

The last petal falls
With a bee hanging on
You walk along
With the wind in your hair
The bears
Have
Gone out with a song.

The sun has gone down
It will rise tomorrow
Without a doubt
Come on, don't
Shout!

Katie Glover (9)
Gatehouse School

THE TIGER

The tiger is a magnificent creature
That lies in the sweltering sun
With such a beautiful look and feature
He waits patiently for his prey to come
Then . . .

Lauren Newman (10)
Gatehouse School

URTHER THE CAT

One night
I looked out
of my window
and I saw my cat.
It was big and black
I saw another cat
It was ginger.
It looked like Urther
But it couldn't be.
I rubbed my eyes but
It still looked like Urther.

Then I thought when
She's in, she's adorable
But when she's out she's a
Demon in disguise.

Jack Kirby (9)
Gatehouse School

CATS

Cats crawl
Softly
Quietly
Down the hall,
Beautiful,
Brown,
Purring
Gently.

Omar Rashid (9)
Gatehouse School

THE TROUBLE WITH BEING THE ELDEST

The trouble with being the eldest is . . .
You cannot choose who's first
But since the day my brothers were born
My life has been under a curse.
Two sisters can annoy your brain
But two brothers are even worse.
Unless they stop their endless fun
I'll end up in a hearse.

Vanessa Albert (11)
Gatehouse School

RIDDLE POEM

Sometimes I'm black, brown or white
To see me you need some light.
Please touch me and say I'm cute
Always talk and don't be mute.

If I find a girl I will fight
I am nocturnal (I am awake in the night)
I love my owners big and small
When I stretch I am tall.

Marie Deenmamode (8)
Gatehouse School

THE ELDERLY

She has straw-like hair and a bendy knee
When she gives me a pat
Her hands are like the claws of a cat.
Her wrinkly skin is very thin and is like old newspaper,
Her eyes once danced as two moonbeams
But now not even a glint has passed the sad look of emptiness
We see which really is nothing more than an empty shadow
That looks to the floor.

Andrew Isaias (10)
Gatehouse School

SNAKE

I'm a green log that moves at night,
I live in a rainforest where I eat and sleep.
I slither about whenever I'm bored,
I can jump off trees, sometimes.
Never underestimate the power of a snake.

Andrew Moodley (10)
Gatehouse School

THE WIND

The wind blows across the floor
The leaves flutter from the trees
The sound of the fluttering leaves
And the blowing wind are everywhere,
The leaves smash here and there.

George Hanness (10)
Gatehouse School

BIRTHDAY GIRL

B undles of surprises
I ncreasing before my eyes
R ich fruit cake
T hat my mother did bake
H appy birthday wishes
D ozens of tasty dishes
A nd I loved the cap
Y ou bought me from Gap

G reat thanks I gave
I was dressed to rave
R ave I did
L ike a little kid.

Rosie Inns (11)
Guardian Angels RC JM & I School

MANDY AND JOSH

Mandy
I have a friend called Mandy,
She looks a bit handy,
She is my friend,
We never pretend
And she loves candy.

Josh
I have a friend called Josh,
He is quite posh,
He is so dumb,
He picks his bum
And never has a wash.

Nicole Campbell (7)
Guardian Angels RC JM & I School

I Saw You

I saw you this morning,
I saw you tonight,
Which made me think,
Oh! What a beautiful sight
I saw you on TV
Which filled me with glee,
But then I thought how can it be,
I'm sure it looked like a flat headed ball.
I didn't know you're really that tall,
Which was quite unusual,
But then I remembered you are beautiful,
Now how can you tell me such a ball,
Could look as beautiful as you and all,
Please do not forget that I saw you this morning,
Then what makes you say that I think you are boring,
I may not see you tomorrow,
But don't you see I'm filled with glee at the sight I saw you today!

Ebisiemen Ajayi (10)
Guardian Angels RC JM & I School

Boxing

Boxing is an age old thing
you sure need guts to get in the ring
sweat and tears
blood and fears
train, train, train for lots of years.

There's lots of famous names I know
but here are just a few to show
Lennox Lewis, Terry Spinx
Charlie Magri, Sammy McCarthy,
but here is one that everyone knows
Cassius Clay the great Muhammed Ali.

Themba Green (10)
Guardian Angels RC JM & I School

Football

Today's the match,
When Brazil gets thrashed,
England is the best,
And Brazil are the pest,
The game starts,
When Heskey runs past,
England wins the toss,
When Beckham gives a
Lovely cross,
England need some goals,
Out comes a player and scores,
Who was it? Paul Scholes!

Ronaldo is just standing still,
When Brazil are losing one nil,
Brazil needs some goals,
Out comes a player and scores
An own goal,
Who was it? Paul Scholes!

Adam Mansoor (10)
Gwyn Jones Primary School

A Life In A Month

January is full of cold
and when you start to feel most old.
February is near to spring
just before the flowers sing.
March is when life awakens
and all the space on earth is taken.
April is most full of showers
stopping every other hour.
May is almost the middle of the year
joy and laughter is all you can hear.
June is the best of all
the month of my birthday has come to call.
July is mostly very hot
when you go outside a lot.
August the end of the summer heat
for the beginning of school you get quite neat.
September is quite very hard
with hardly any time to play in the yard.
October when you have settled in
it was funny when Sir sat on a pin.
November is when you can hardly wait
for Christmas and for Christmas cake.
December is a happy time
When you sing poems that always rhyme.

The seasons have good times and bad
but the times I have are always mad.

Alice Claussen (10)
Gwyn Jones Primary School

NATURE!

The world goes round and round,
with lots of life in the ground,
and lots of things in the sea,
for you and me to see.
Please don't ruin nature
for the people of the future,
And please, please, please,
don't cut down the trees.
Think of the bird's nest
and all of the rest.
The days go cold,
and animals grow old.
Forests, rainforests
Parks, ponds
and even your garden are
animals' habitats.
Just as you care for cats, dogs and even little frogs.
Just please care for them,
We're big and they're small,
So please care for them all.

Indiana Richard (10)
Gwyn Jones Primary School

WHY?

Why are we here?
Why are we here?
Are we the first
Or are we the last?
Are we alone in this
Cosmic universe
Or are we not? . . .

Christopher Waddington (10)
Gwyn Jones Primary School

THE MAN IN THE DUMP

The man in the dump
Hits with a thump
He asked to play
So say OK.

He sang with a singer
He plays with his finger
He went to the loo
When we all said, 'Boo'

He says hi with a ting
His name is Minging
He's la da da
We're bla bla bla.

He sits in a trolley
We all call him Wally
He sat on a bee
When we jumped in the sea.

He has a one dollar
His neighbour's Miss Waller
He plays on the bay
Hip hip hooray

His nickname is Dopey
His wife's head is slopey
He plays with his toes
Which smelled like a rose.

His wife is quite nutty
His mother is sooty
The fly said hi but
We shall now say goodbye.

Laura Waller (10)
Gwyn Jones Primary School

DRAGON, DRAGON

Dragon, dragon soaring high,
Dragon, dragon why won't you die?
Dragon, dragon in my mind,
Dragon, dragon not too kind.

Dragon, dragon killing why?
Dragon, dragon it's not shy.
Dragon, dragon burning now,
Dragon, dragon that smells foul.

Jaylan Konrad-Lee (11)
Gwyn Jones Primary School

BEING AT SCHOOL IS SO UNCOOL!

I snore and snore
It's such a bore
My eyes drop closed
I kick my toes
The boys all giggle chat, chat, chat
I click my pencil, tap, tap, tap.
Being at school is so uncool!
I can't be bothered with all this work
and our class teacher's such a jerk.
The clever kids all get good grades
sour grapes is what they say
Being at school is so uncool!
Finally a good part of the day
when we can go out and have a play.
We go back in it's so unfair
I know what I'll do I'll play with my hair.
The teacher is watching, he's really hairy
I run outside to have some fun and
guess who's there, hooray it's *Mum!*

Shannon Maher (10)
Gwyn Jones Primary School

LITTLE BROTHERS

I was walking down the road one day
Why?
'Cause I was going to my friends
Why?
I wanted to have some fun
Why?
So I could get away from *you*
Why?
So I wanted to be alone
Why?
'Cause you're annoying
Why?
'Cause you are
Why?
    Klabash!
What?

Uwais Qasmi (10)
Gwyn Jones Primary School

SATURDAY'S COOL

Saturday's cool
'Cause there's no school
Like to laze around on the merry-go-round
Don't need no school
When we can be in the pool
My best friends call
Before we go to the mall
Saturday's cool
'Cause there's no school.

Shireen Loonat (11)
Gwyn Jones Primary School

I'VE SEEN A TALKING CAT!

I've seen a talking cat
The cat was small and magical
and very, very beautiful.
At the time she was chasing a rat.

The cat got up and said to the rat,
'Come here I want you for my dinner!'
It took time and at the time the cat was
getting thinner.

Then I saw the reach of a paw
I shouted, 'Please little cat leave that rat,
You don't want him for your dinner.'
'I didn't mean to hurt that rat but I'm a cat.'
That's when I saw the talking cat!

Amber Wilks (11)
Gwyn Jones Primary School

HAPPINESS

Happiness is going on holiday
Happiness is playing football
Happiness is watching sports
Happiness is practising other sorts
Happiness is seeing Arsenal beat Manchester United.

Happiness is my family
Happiness is my friends
Happiness is every day being my birthday!

Zeke Bruney (10)
Gwyn Jones Primary School

THERE GOES ANOTHER ONE

They go zooming past,
Wheels spinning,
Rubber burning,
People watching,
Engine screaming,
Weaving in and out of traffic,
Wobbles so dangerous,
Looks like crashing,
Bang, boom, bang
People stared,
Oil everywhere,
Driver's dead,
End another person's life.

Matthew Harvey (10)
Gwyn Jones Primary School

THE EAGLE

Soaring through the sky
Spreading it's beautiful wings
Squawking as it flies.

Drifting in the air,
Searching, hunting for its prey
The eagle is here.

Swoops down to the ground
Stretches out its sharp talons
Snatches at its prey.

Thomas Keirle (10)
Gwyn Jones Primary School

MY FAMILY

Makes funny noises,
Snores and then pauses,
Football mania,
Bad behaviour,
And that's what I call my dad!

Cooking mania,
Stress behaviour,
Always in a mess,
She's a natural disaster,
And that's what I call my
Aunt Bess.

Emma Tye (10)
Gwyn Jones Primary School

A TIGER IS...

A tiger is...
    a living creature
    its fur is its best feature
    its tail sways side to side
    its mouth will open wide
    its prey
    will have to run away
    its legs run really fast
    its prey will have to try and last.

Rebecca Boot (10)
Gwyn Jones Primary School

IN THE SWIMMING POOL

People splashing
People bashing
In the swimming pool.
Laughing, joking,
Having fun,
In the swimming pool.

Now comes the wave machine
Bump, bump!
Bash, bash!
That's the wave machine.

People in the deep end
People big and small
People with their goggles on
Underwater they go.

In another half an hour
People are going to have a shower
Dry themselves
Get their clothes off the shelf.

People leaving.

Ella O'Donnell (8)
Handsworth Primary School

THE MUCKY POTION

Double, double, toil and trouble
One slice of frogs' legs and twenty-two pegs
A tiny piece of frogs' breath and a bird in death.
Two sets of cows' horns and thirty-four thorns.
Six horses' eyes and twenty-four flies.
One piece of hair and sixty-two dares.

A piece of body and lots of code.
Eye of newt and a little of flute.
Rattle of a rattlesnake and some water of a lake.
Two bats' wings and lots of things.
Double, double, toil and trouble
So come on make me a potion!

Georgina Hurlock (9)
Handsworth Primary School

SCARECROW

I'm a scarecrow,
I save all the crops
I'm still in the field
When the last leaf drops.

I watch all the wheat grow
I see all the corn
I see them at dusk,
I watch them at dawn.

I have really old clothes,
I'm a man-shaped birdhouse,
In my heart there's a swallow,
In my shoe there's a mouse.

I've a dreadfully dull duty
Tied to a stick.
Just scaring the birds,
(They fly off quite quick).

When you celebrate harvest,
Think of everyone
If you have food
Then my work is done.

Alice Butcher (11)
Handsworth Primary School

TEACHERS

Teachers, teachers, teachers

Chattering aloud telling children off . . . then acting proud.

Teachers, teachers, teachers

Hate children a lot eating in the middle of class then losing the plot.

Teachers, teachers, teachers

Make you miss play and make you clean their dirty tray.

Teachers, teachers, teachers

Are nasty creatures, will they change?
I don't think so . . . *Never! Ever!*

Teachers, teachers, teachers!

Are very loud and have a big crowd!
And are proud.

Jahmel Perkins (9)
Handsworth Primary School

MY WORLD

My world you cannot see
Because it's underneath a tree
My world is great
You will have at least one mate.

My world is fun
With a yummy bun
My world we have news
But we don't refuse.

My world is free
We even have a sea
My world is nice
We always give each other advice.

My world is cool
We have lots of beach balls
My world is so secret
You won't find me.

Caroline Harvey (9)
Handsworth Primary School

SAVE THE TREES

When autumn comes I go bald and cold.
So what will keep me warm?
The tree said.
The berries
But the birds come and peck them especially the cherries.

What happens when the cat comes and scratches me?
The tree said.
Don't worry, the wind will blow them away
But what happens when it's a windless day?

What happens when my fruit is gone, what will the animals eat?
The tree said.
Meat!
But that's not what birds eat.

But what happens when the axe comes?
The tree said.
Run!

Yasmin Cromwell (11)
Handsworth Primary School

THE FLOWER

You start off with a tiny seed,
Now what else do you need?
A pot, some soil, water in a pan,
Or how about a watering can?

Now fill the pot with soil,
Sprinkle seeds sparkling like foil,
Water it a little
Go away and eat a skittle.

Come back in a day,
The seeds will have gone away,
In their place will be,
Green sprouts sitting beautifully.

After more than a week,
You will begin to freak,
They will not have grown,
You will begin to moan.

Get on the phone,
To the greenhouse all alone,
Cry, cry, cry and cry,
Your flowers are about to die.

Abbie Lunn (9)
Handsworth Primary School

SCHOOL

At school we have a class rule
Everyone who does not obey the rule
would have to drink water from the swimming pool.
I don't act like one of those fools.
Some people even get chucked onto the naughty stool.
Those cool fools had to fix a clock with a tool.

Hardly anyone does enough work because they eat pies
for dinner and then I go around saying it's not wise to eat pies,
it dries and dies out your brain.

Other people like school but I think school drools!

Pavan Chamdal (9)
Handsworth Primary School

IN THE HAUNTED, HAUNTED HOUSE

In the haunted, haunted house,
there was a very spooky ghost
who always sat on a rough log.

In the haunted, haunted house,
there is a skeleton with
cobwebs all over it.

In the haunted, haunted house
they had a table which
was made of cobwebs and skeletons.

In the haunted, haunted house
there were beds made out of
cobwebs and skeletons for the pillows.

In the haunted, haunted house
everything was made
of skeletons and cobwebs.

Anna Panayi (8)
Handsworth Primary School

WHERE THE DOLPHINS LEAP

Down in the deep
Where the dolphins leap
Under the sea
Where you can be
Down in the deep
Where the dolphins leap.

Down in the deep
Where the whales leap
Under the sea
Where we can be
Down in the deep
Where the whales leap.

Down in the deep
Where the dolphins leap
And the whales leap
Under the sea
Where all of us can be
Down in the deep
Where the dolphins leap.

Annie Hutchinson (8)
Handsworth Primary School

WAR

The world will be ready for war
But we hope we never will
One word the world dreads
People who go in and never come out
People who go in and die
Lucky some will survive
One word that means a lot, *war*

Alexander Baker (8)
Handsworth Primary School

IN THE ZOO

In the zoo
In the zoo
What do the animals do?
They can eat fruit
They can eat leaves
Animals are asleep
Nice and good
But the animals cry and I don't know why
My animal does not cry and I don't know why
So I get my dad and what does he say
We have to go
So home and away
So I did not play

In the zoo.

Sian Barrett (8)
Handsworth Primary School

HOMELESS

Children are homeless,
They get no toys,
Children suffer.

They starve,
They are homeless,
Children survive.

The children go to a orphanage
They go home with a family,
They are not homeless.

Oliver Barker (8)
Handsworth Primary School

THE STREET MAN

The street man goes all around streets
nicking all the people's sweets.

The street man hides in the alley
on Lee Valley.

The street man goes around the shops
eating all the cocopops.

He goes in the street
eating some mincemeat.

The street man goes around the streets
eating on all the dumped seats.

Samuel Smith (8)
Handsworth Primary School

BAT

In the night I fly freely being followed by only my shadow.
My darkened wings let me soar above the stars where I cannot
                                                          be disturbed.
I flit at the sight of blood but I am considered still to be an evil
                                                          creature of the night.
For I am a bloodsucking myth, a beastly legend.
My bony face craves fruit, not death, not blood, not darkness.
I sleep through the noise of day waiting, waiting to be free again.

Michael Carroll (10)
Handsworth Primary School

A DREAM OF A CHILD IN TANZANIA
DREAM, DREAM

Dream, dream
Hope that tomorrow will be better than today,
We'll have clean water and be able to play,
Dream, dream,
Life will change and hopefully now families won't die from the lack of water,
We'll have proper toilets and education for every son and daughter,
Dream, dream,
Not having to walk ten miles every day of our lives,
We'll be able to live proper lives being able to survive,
Dream, dream.

Somar Ibrahim (10)
Larkswood Junior School

WATER

W ater travels all around the world
A ll water can be clean or dirty
T he people in Tanzania and Uganda need clean water
E veryone in the world needs clean, fresh water
R eally nice people should give water to other homes to help them stay alive
And healthy.

Lana Heath (9)
Larkswood Junior School

THINK ABOUT PEOPLE WHO NEED WATER

T anzania and Uganda need clean water, think how sad they are
H ealthy water we drink, just think how unhealthy their water is
I nfections and other illnesses, effects to their body system
N ice blue water we have, but nasty, dirty waterholes they've got
K ind water that doesn't kill us, but two countries whose water is deadly.

A nger from parents because their familes are dying
B abies need clean water to live and mothers are worried
O pen the door to a better life
U nhappy people are just asking for clean water
T hey are not so fortunate like we are, please try to help.

P eople have to walk ten miles to the nearest waterhole
E nd to illness
O nly a bucket to last for a day
P eople are going to be grateful if we help
L ife is special, please do not make it feel like a dump
E ager others, to help is not too much

W hat better lives they could have with clean water
H elp is essential, show your kindness
O pen their smiles again

N o more dying, much more surviving
E nd the selfishness
E nergy and calcium are important to our bodies
D ying is sad, agree with us and think that they should have longer lives

W ater is necessary
A ll they're trying to achieve is clean water
T hirst can be dangerous
E nd contaminated water
R aise money, give it to Blue Peter and the people in Tanzania and Uganda will have clean water supplies.

Vanessa Regresado (10)
Larkswood Junior School

TANZANIA AND UGANDA

People, people in Uganda and Tanzania are helpless
have to walk miles and miles for a waterhole.

People, people in Uganda and Tanzania can't live
without water.

People, people in Uganda and Tanzania need your
help, could you help them?

People, people in Uganda and Tanzania usually die
because they have dirty water or they get a disease.

People, people in Uganda and Tanzania are very
unlucky, think about you having clean water and they haven't.

People, people in Uganda and Tanzania say they are
unhappy, they will say please help me.

People, people in Uganda and Tanzania.

Reade Mulvany (9)
Larkswood Junior School

THE LIVING WORLD

Plants and trees,
Whistling through the wind.
See the seeds scatter,
Carried by the wind.
Birds in flight
Swooping up and down,
Pecking up the seeds,
that fall upon the ground.
Down comes the rain
and seeds start to grow,
soon comes the summer
and flowers put on a show.
All too soon
the flowers begin to die.
The wind whips up again
And away the birds will fly.

Thomas Purver (10)
Larkswood Junior School

POLLUTION POEM

P lacing its poison on perfect land
O vertaking rivers and seas
L iving creatures live no more
L akes turn blue to black
U nder the water fish die
T aking over our land
I llnesses begin
O ur lives destroyed
N o longer we live.

Esme Humphries-King (10)
Larkswood Junior School

THEY NEED YOUR HELP

There are lots of poor people,
All over our world,
With dirty brown water,
Their crops are all curled,
Their food is all spoiled,
You can't make some tea,
The water's not boiled.

Do you fancy walking,
For eight or ten miles?
Or hours or weeks?
Or days as well?
Then help and save,
The lives of the poor,
With everybody's money,
Mine and yours.

Jacqueline Kilikita (10)
Larkswood Junior School

MY POEM

Hot dusty days and aching feet.
From walking in the midday heat.
Dirty water in the well.
Making everything stale and smell.
People dying from disease.
We can help this problem ease.
Water in a well can be a reality.
Clean water for all a must, not a possibility.

Nicola Morris (10)
Larkswood Junior School

ACT NOW

U ganda is a very poor country,
G etting water is very hard.
A ll the people have to walk ten miles to get clean water,
N one of them have drink water.
D oing things in Uganda is hard because they have no money,
A nd we can help.

A ll people can help,
N one of them will survive,
D on't let them suffer any more.

T anzania is in the same situation,
A ll they need is money.
N ow is the time to act,
Z oom into action
A nd if we act now we will help people,
N obody should have to live this way . . .
I t is very cruel,
A *ct now!*

Harry Kane (9)
Larkswood Junior School

THE LIVING WORLD

We go to the stream
to get some water,
to wash and make us clean
we travel for each and every day
the stream is so far away.

The water is dirty, never clean
we need to survive,
if we had clean water,
it would help us stay alive.

So please support us with your donation
and help us give water to a nation.
It would be great, what a dream
to drink pure water and stay clean.

Charlie Clayton (9)
Larkswood Junior School

DIRTY WATER!

The people in Tanzania and Uganda,
Very, very sick,
Live without water
How can they exist?
Ten miles and back again,
To the nearest water hole
Must be exhausting.

To do all that walking
But we have been watching TV
About a Blue Peter Appeal
All about water
I have been thinking of making a deal
And if we could raise some money
By selling some cakes
Just for twenty pence.

What a difference it would make
We try and try
So these people do not die
Please buy our cakes
For goodness sake.

Tom Frater (9)
Larkswood Junior School

DROUGHT AND STARVATION

D rought is everlasting
R ivers and lakes run dry
O nly scarce supplies of water left
U nderground they have to dig
G irls and boys travel miles a day
H ope is never far away
T ired and hungry they return.

A lways dry
N ever wet
D irty water everywhere

S ick children getting worse
T ime runs shorter like a curse
A ll they need is time and help
R unning water is their dream
V egetation food and grain
A ll is possible if we help
T able-top sales raise money fast
I magine a way that you could help
O nce they get the money, the work can begin.
N ice days can be had in Tanzania again.

Regan Fielder (10)
Larkswood Junior School

UGANDA AND TANZANIA

Uganda and Tanzania need help
No clean water, even dirty when it's far away
Walking with a bottle on their head.
This has to stop, there has to be another way.

Water pumps is what they need
Any size or colour
Water is what they're going to need
To the children weak and poor.

Help by finding money
Any amount will do
To provide pumps, hygiene
And a proper loo.

Fiona Hynds (9)
Larkswood Junior School

MAN VS ANIMAL

Man has poisoned your water supply,
will this cause you to die?
Go fight man, remember to hide,
Don't let them kill you for your hide,
Your number is falling but don't give in or
else you will become extinct,
Go to the edge of the Earth and run to a
safe place,
There it is good for you, so don't let me
down,
Please, oh please don't let me down!
Come let us go and get out of here with me
and your friends,
Where it is calm and peaceful not like here,
When men come and their guns go *bang!*
In our bodies,
Your food is being knocked down to the
ground,
Homes are built on your land no longer a
paradise park.
Come, let's run, run, run, run, run!

Samuel Verdin (10)
Larkswood Junior School

BLUE PETER APPEAL

Villages in Uganda have no rain.
This is such a pain.

No water to drink
and you would think
that as a nation
what is needed is education.

The water here smells quite rank.
There is no luxury water tank.
Forget about the kitchen sinks.
The water here, always stinks.

So this is an appeal.
Help these people have a decent meal.

Raise some money for a good cause.
Help Ugandan people have a hygienic water source.

Jason Maduro (10)
Larkswood Junior School

TANZANIA AND UGANDA

W hat a disaster for some poor countries
A lways drinking dirty water.
T en miles' walk from all their homes.
E ager people not wanting to walk ten miles.
R uined because of a bad disease.

Georgie Yianni (10)
Larkswood Junior School

THIRSTY KIRSTY

There was a girl called Kirsty
She woke up and was thirsty
Her life was hell
As it was ten miles to the well
She put the pot on her head
Like her mother said.

The water was dirty day after day
As much as they tried they could
Not keep the disease at bay
A pump, a pump for clean water she needs
Before the disease breeds and breeds.

Blue Peter, Blue Peter, our life is not hell
Now that we don't have to walk to the well.

George Powell (10)
Larkswood Junior School

WATER

Water can be hot,
Water can be cold,
Water can be dangerous and also fun.

Water, water everywhere
On the ground, in the air,
Out the taps and in the bath.

You can drink and wash with it,
Keep the plants and fish alive.

Water is a precious gift.

Kane Slisz (9)
Larkswood Junior School

WATER WILL HELP

W ater will help those people who suffer.
A ll of those people have no proper water supplies.
T he toilets are not hygienic.
E veryone suffers.
R aising money will help those people who suffer.

W ill they ever drink clean healthy water again?
I n seventy-four villages something hopefully will change
L ands struck with diseases
L ands of crying people

H oles with water in are far away
E very type of person in both countries suffer
L ands drying up
P umps are needed for water underground.

Billie Poppy (10)
Larkswood Junior School

WATER WORKS APPEAL

W ater Works Appeal.
A well is what the people need,
T anzania and Uganda need your help,
E veryone should send some money,
R ain, rain it never comes.

W ater Works Appeal,
O rganise a Bring and Buy sale *now!*
R aid your piggy banks,
K ind are those to spare a penny,
S o help Blue Peter to reach their target.

Mitchell House (9)
Larkswood Junior School

CAN YOU LIVE WITHOUT WATER? NO!

I wash my face
My big brother cleans his teeth
My little brother has a shower
My mum waters her plants
My dad washes his car
We all have breakfasts
With a glass of water
In some countries like
Uganda and Tanzania
Don't have water to
Do the things we do every
Day, it is a *torture!*

Katie Goodland (10)
Larkswood Junior School

WATER WORKS

W alking
A bout
T en miles, people need
E nough clean and safe water to survive
R unning and

W alking
O ver some
R ocky ground
K ind people, who care about others, we need
S ome support.

Jonathan Palmer (10)
Larkswood Junior School

HOPE

Sometimes we get so caught up in our lives that we don't think about any other.
So it's time for us to help make a change, surely we should bother.
They have hardly any food, little education and for clean water we're talking miles.
So it can't be hard to help just a little to bring back all their smiles.
The sun is hot, there's diseases and dying, all around the children are crying.
The parents frown as there is nothing that can be done, they want to be able to have fun under the sun.
There would be nothing better than to think that they can be happy and cheer
So let's raise some money for Uganda and Tanzania.

Nikki Drewett (10)
Larkswood Junior School

MY POEM

U nless we raise enough money they will keep dying.
G etting water for them is very important.
A mount of money needed is £500,000.
N obody knows how they feel inside.
D on't take our water for granted.
A sk yourself what your life would be like in that country?

Think of the people in Uganda and Tanzania next time you drink!

Sam Hollis (10)
Larkswood Junior School

WATER, WATER EVERYWHERE

People walk ten miles a day,
to fetch their water in this strange way.
The water is not clean, the children get ill,
Why don't they get help from us who are well?

So we must try to help them so they can say,
'Life for us is safer this way.'
Help them to help themselves,
to expand their water and make more wells.

They will learn and make their country better,
so children can grow up stronger and fitter.

Charis Thoma (9)
Larkswood Junior School

JUST LIKE ME!

I looked in the mirror and I saw me,
But there was someone else moving around that looked like me,
I said who are you?
But she said who are you?
So I jumped up and down,
But she turned around and around.
So I said goodbye,
But she never replied,
So why is she here?
Why won't she disappear.

Monique Ventour (11)
Longshaw Primary School

My Grandad

It's been a year that he's been gone,
It's been a sad time but life goes on.
I really miss his cheeky smile,
But I don't miss those cigarette butts that smelt for a long while.
The ashtray is empty,
So is the bin because that's where he pilled his betting slips in.
If there is a Heaven I'm sure you're there,
Sitting in your favourite chair.
You're most probably passing wind like you don't care,
Don't get carried away and please don't forget to spray your hair.
I know that Heaven's not that far away,
But I'll probably see you there another day.
I'm still missing you a real lot,
And we're looking after your flowers in your flowerpot.
And I will miss you for as long as I'm here,
And every March the 18th I will shed a tear.

Amber Zakrzewski (11)
Longshaw Primary School

I Miss You

I miss you
Like the sun misses the flower
Like the sun misses the flower in the
Depths of winter
Like the frozen world you have
Banished me to
Like no light may look upon you.

Jack Button (10)
Longshaw Primary School

VISIT TO THE SWIMMING POOL

Going through the crocodile gate
Changing rooms as noisy as the busy road
Banging lockers sound like angry giants
Lifeguards shouting, whistles blowing
Toddlers' armbands hold them up magically in the water
Babies scream like buses' brakes
Having lots of fun
Making lots of friends
Lights shine down mirror balls
Diving and gliding through the water
Front crawl arms swing like windmills
Breaststroke legs like a giant frog
Making the water move like the sea
Swirling round and round in a forward roll
Oh, water up your nose
Getting dry in a nice warm towel
Hairdryers like dragon's breath
I've had a lovely time at the pool.

Philippa McAnulty (10)
Longshaw Primary School

FOOTIE FANATIC

I'm a footie fanatic,
I've got posters on my wall,
I hate mathematics,
I think it's so uncool,
My mum is always bugging me,
To improve my work at school,
My dad is on the phone to me,
Telling me she is cruel!

Francesca Astin Herrera (10)
Longshaw Primary School

MY FRIENDS

Stephanie talks about cats,
Cats, cats, cats.
Cats that go in and out of flaps,
And when it comes to chats,
She always talks about *cats!*

Anoushka talks about squirrels,
Squirrels, squirrels, squirrels.
Squirrels that hold quarrels
And when they come up to me (the squirrels)
They make me laugh because it *tickles.*

Well, I talk about snakes,
Snakes, snakes, snakes,
Snakes that don't look like cakes
The most cutest snakes
So what I talk about is *snakes!*

Martin talks about alligators
Alligators, alligators, alligators.
Alligators that are traitors,
They look like illustrators.
All Martin talks about is *alligators!*

Richard talks about puppies,
Puppies, puppies, puppies.
Puppies that are fluffy,
All cute and cuddly puppies
So Richard always talks about *puppies!*

Callum Kousoulou (10)
Longshaw Primary School

SEASONS

Winter
snow and ice
all looks nice
jumpers, hats and scarves
to keep us warm when we're cold
for all the winter days.

Spring
snow melts
flowers grow
the sun begins to shine
all trees blossom
people drink lots of wine.

Summer
the sun is shining in the sky
school is out
time to go away
buckets and spades
bikinis on
what a way to play.

Autumn
flowers droop
leaves begin to drop
cold wind blowing
rivers flowing
soon it will be snowing.

Anna-Maria Katsimigos (9)
Longshaw Primary School

MY IMAGINATION

I imagine a purple and blue cat,
Sitting on a table, with the Mad Hatter's hat.

I imagine the alphabet without the B,
And money growing on trees.

I imagine free trips to Mars,
And someone inventing cool camera bars.

I imagine no school,
And winter days that are cool.

I imagine that everyone has horses,
And that everyone has different colour sauces.

It's weird how much you can imagine in a blink,
But I can imagine more with a wink.

Natalie Mills (10)
Longshaw Primary School

TEACHERS

Teachers, teachers
What a load of ugly creatures.
Stand up straight,
Don't lean on the wall!
Why are you running in the dinner hall?

Amy, Yasmin, Emily too
You do know you're wearing one odd shoe.

Hakuna Matata have a wonderful day
That's what I wish they would say.

Amy Barnes (10)
Longshaw Primary School

The Dream

The dream I had was ever so clear
Angels playing golden harps
And then I saw him standing there
Smiling the smile he used to smile.
He was standing on a golden cloud
Which was so fluffy.
He pointed me out to Jesus
Jesus smiled and said, 'Welcome my child.'
He beckoned me to meet the Lord God.
I saw God, the Father Almighty and bowed.
The dream I had was ever so clear,
Tonight I saw my dear uncle,
My dear Uncle Wayne.

Lauren Cadogan (9)
Longshaw Primary School

My Dream

As I was walking in my dream
I heard a loud scream
I walked towards the scream I heard.

There stood so still
a person on the floor.
The person she was dying
She said to me she did
pass this poem on
for all to hear
that's what she said
lying on the floor.

Zoe Scicluna (9)
Longshaw Primary School

UNDER THE SEA

Under the unknown sea,
There is a mysterious castle,
Look over there it's a glistening key,
Inside that special parcel.

Under the unknown sea,
The dolphin leaps,
The turtle creeps,
There's a happy seal
And an electric eel.

Under the unknown sea,
There is a mysterious castle,
Look over there it's a glistening key,
Inside that special parcel.

Sonia Soomessur (11)
Longshaw Primary School

ROBIN HOOD

Robin Hood and his merry band,
Once owned a lot of land.
One day when Norman barons came
they took their swords and began to aim.
When they thought they would never last
they fled to the wood extremely fast.
Now they wear olive-green
and hide to camouflage, so they can't be seen.

Abbie Loman (11)
Longshaw Primary School

EARLY MORNINGS

I set my alarm for 7am
to get up every day.
Just to go to school in the morning,
but tired in every way.

I have an early start in the morning,
starting my work at nine.
Even though I've been awake for a while,
I'm still not feeling fine.

Half the day's gone by already,
having break at 10am.
I can't believe it's still so early,
wish it was pm!

Richard Brown (10)
Longshaw Primary School

MY IMAGINARY FRIEND

My imaginary friend,
She can jump as high as the moon.
She can dance like a fairy,
And is as light as a balloon.

She can swim the English Channel,
She is very strong indeed.
She can also run kilometres,
She's a magical friend for me,
She's my imaginary friend.

Emily Nichols (10)
Longshaw Primary School

UG

Ug
Ug
Ug
lives
under
the
plug
not in the bedroom
or
under the rug
and if he grips you
in his icy hug
final words
will be
    glug glug glug.

Rojdan Gul (11)
Longshaw Primary School

MY BEDROOM

My bedroom is pink
but sometimes is full of ink.
My friends come round
and mess up the place.
I say, 'What a mess!'
then I get very crazy.
My mum says, 'Tidy it up,'
but I am too lazy.

Shanice Attram (9)
Longshaw Primary School

ICE CREAM SUNDAE

It's the ice cream sundae
What a joy to eat
It is something that nothing
Else can beat!

I love the chocolate sauce
And the cherry on top
But when I can't have my sundae
I always get in a strop!

Yasmin Halil (10)
Longshaw Primary School

OUR IMAGINATION

Our imagination is a butterfly,
An airborne purple mist.
A land of white summery clouds,
And turrets all in a twist.

Our imagination are moons and stars,
In our hearts and in our minds,
A thought which lives in us all,
Love and joy combined.

Anoushka Russell (10)
Longshaw Primary School

THE CRACK ON THE DOOR

The crack on the door
made a star on the floor.
it shone very bright like
a beautiful sunlight.

Rippley Gallagher (9)
Longshaw Primary School

LIFE

Life is complicated sometimes,
If you're in doubt,
Be sure to work it out,
If you're looking for an answer,
You've got to find it deep down
where it counts,
Life isn't made for arguing all the time,
So we should all stop taking it out
on other people.

Bonnie Wingfield (10)
Longshaw Primary School

THE VALENTINE DAY

The Valentine day has just begun
Get a kiss from your lovely one.
Valentine's Day is full of love
It makes you think of up above
Then you see something fly by
It looks like a lovely butterfly.

Stephanie Karagiannidis (9)
Longshaw Primary School

THE RAINBOW

Rainbows have colours from the sun
It makes you feel like you're the only one
We never know what's at the end of the rainbow
Because it disappears
That's the colourful rainbow that's been near Earth
All these years.

Jade Nash (9)
Longshaw Primary School

MY SILLY SISTER

My silly sister
sitting by the sea,
eating her lollipop
playing with the sand
making a sandcastle
and knocking it
down.

Prima Patel (9)
Longshaw Primary School

WORDS

Bright is the ring of words
When the right man rings them.
Fair the fall of songs
When the singer sings them.
Still they are carolled and said,
On wings they are carried.
After the singer is dead, and the maker buried.

Sasha Robinson-King (10)
Longshaw Primary School

CAT

Green eyes
Oblivious to darkness
Treading through the undergrowth on velvet paws
Sniffing the air
The scent of darkness
Fallen upon the Earth
Like a star-eaten blanket protecting the world from evil and wrong.

Stephanie Smith (10)
Longshaw Primary School

I SAW AN ELEPHANT

I saw an elephant
walking down the street,
I thought it was cute so I gave
it a treat, it screamed in my ear, I
started to fear,
and at the end it said, 'Are you
OK my dear?'

I took it to my house
he caught a mouse.
He got scared,
but it was a dare,
I said, 'Sorry
bye-bye
I am going away
in a lorry!'

Uroosa Malik (9)
Monega Primary School

KITTEN WISE

My little cat is black and white
When I go to bed she sleeps with me all night.

When I get up she follows me around
Makes a funny noise like a purring sound.

She plays with a ball around the house
I think she imagines it's a little mouse.

She likes to go in the garden to chase a bee
The antics she does is funny to see.

She cries for her dinner and has meat and cheese
She would sooner do this than chase the bees.

She then curls up and goes to sleep
I don't want to wake her so I creep.

Hazara Khatun (10)
Monega Primary School

FLOWERS

The Earth is full of attractive flowers,
Swaying in the wind, waiting for bees.
Blowing all away, the petals indeed.

Blossoms every summer,
Dies every winter,
Turns from one vivid colour to a dull colour.

Bees buzzing into pollen,
From one flower to another,
Flowers are street lights to us.

Rohoney Ravi (11)
Monega Primary School

THE FUTURE

The sky will be darkened by the
Wings of many flying cars.
Children going on trips;
To Mars.
Debris and masonry flood
The streets.
Robot bands singing
Teens clapping the back beats
Holiday tickets being booked
For the moon!
Panicking people:
'Aliens invading us soon!'
World maps have
Altered once again,
The continents have moved
A kilometre of ten!
Our solar system now consists
Of five new planets:
Tilanus, Sytos, Rigi
Famini and Prets.
New animals exist,
There is one called a Zore!
And, *hey kids . . .*
    . . . school exists no more! . . .

Iftikhar Ahmed (11)
Monega Primary School

GHOSTS

I'd like to be a ghost, I would,
To be a ghost is cool.
For ghosts don't have to go to work
And ghosts don't have to go to school.

A ghost can stay up late at night
(In fact they always do)
And ghosts get rooms all to themselves
By simply shouting, 'Whoooooooo!'

Nazish Mahmood (11)
Monega Primary School

JAGUAR

Jaguars are fierce
They come out at night
To catch their prey.

Yellow eyes and a big grin
Animals beware of the danger ahead.

A black body and a skinny tail
It is not to be seen
And not to be heard
For it comes out at night
When the danger arrives.

Sharp teeth and a large mouth
To kill the victims
That lie in its way.

Large paws and big claws
Ready to catch the next victim
Of the night.

Shahhan Spall (11)
Monega Primary School

MOONLIGHT

The moon is blue and it gives us light,
Look closer and you will see it's bright.
It does not come out during the day,
It comes out its own way, in the lack of light.

Its place next to the wonderful stars,
They move around without a sound,
The sun and moon are friends,
Every day they have turns.

Whenever it's noon the sun rises,
And it shines on us with the sun,
To give us a delightful sunny
And also a cheerful day.

Whenever it's evening the sunset and the moon come out,
To give a pleasant view with its beautiful curved-shape body.
Moonlight is nature, moonlight gives us light,
It's bright and it shines on us.

Kemi Quadri (11)
Monega Primary School

WHY?

Why is the Earth round?
Why do we need hands?
Why are people rich?
Why do we have bands?

Why is three the magic number?
Why do we need the loo?
Why do we have names
like Mike, Sally and Sue?

Why are you asking so many questions?
You may say
I am too young to know
There's more to learn than yesterday.

Shahina Rahman (11)
Monega Primary School

AT THE CORNER SHOP

Chocolate doughnuts,
Sticky sweets,
Strawberry lace
And messy treats.

> Toffee apples,
> Sugar mice,
> Marshmallows,
> All things nice.

Cola bottles,
Bubblegum,
More and more,
Yum, yum, yum!

> Chocolate buttons,
> Fizzy pop,
> Buy it all
> At the shop!

Thasnima Begum (10)
Monega Primary School

THERE WERE TEN LITTLE FOOTBALLERS

There were ten little footballers playing in the field,
One fell down and hurt his head.
There were nine little footballers, playing in the field,
One said, 'Hey,' and the other one fell in the clay.
There were eight little footballers, playing in the field
One said, 'Hi,' and the other one said, 'bye'.
There were seven little footballers playing in the field
One fell down and broke his leg.
There were six little footballers playing in the field
One said, 'Look,' and the other one fell onto a crook.
There were five little footballers playing in the field
One said, 'Bee,' and the other one fell onto a tree.
There were four little footballers playing in the field
One said, 'Five,' and the other one looked through the hive.
There were three little footballers playing in the field
One sang a song and the other one fell into the pond.
There were two little footballers playing in the field
One said, 'Goal,' and the other one fell in the hole.
There was one little footballer playing in the field
One said, 'I won.'

Sajna Mitha Choudhury (10)
Monega Primary School

THE NIGHT

Nobody knows why the night goes by,
In the cloudy, cloudy, cloudy sky.
Gather the stars to see the moon,
'Have a look at the king!' they would say, then,
Together, they would run from the coming day.

Judita Jasiunaite (10)
Monega Primary School

SPACE!

I was looking out in the window and wished I was in space,
But I was at home and I was in a big disgrace.

Then I saw a shooting star,
I wished I were on a rocket quite far.

Mercury, Venus, I wanted to explore,
But my heart kept on saying I wanted more.

Then I looked up at the sky and saw the moon,
My heart started to play a lovely tune!

When I woke up I found it was a dream,
And everyone downstairs started to scream!

I was in my room, I was really sad,
I looked up in space and I saw my . . . *dad!*

Husnain Nasim (9)
Monega Primary School

I LOVE CATS

Have you seen my cat?
My big fat cat who sat
On a mat and wore a purple hat,
Eating a big smelly rat.
But now she's gone,
So what can I do
But wait, wait the bell's rang.
Surprise, here's your beautiful old cat,
And now we are going to have a miaow, miaow chat!

Amina Gull (9)
Monega Primary School

TEACHER'S SPELL TO MAKE THE CLASS PASS

First she gets her witch's hat,
And puts inside a PE bat,
Then she adds a few Pritt Sticks
And a piece of work which she ticks.
A cup of tea which has gone cold
Better still if there's a lot of mould!
Mixed with that some maths worksheets
From a photocopier that overheats
She then throws in with her bare hands
Last week's numeracy and literacy plans
And finally squeezing in all her PVA glue
She cackles, 'My spell will get them through.'
But that was not all
She forgot the salt.

Kayrul Mirza (10)
Monega Primary School

PETS - I LOVE PETS

Pets are great, pets are fun,
Some pets you can take for a run.
A pet can be anything you want.
A dog, a cat, even both.
A snake, crocodile, rhino, hippo,
A kangaroo, an elephant, a dolphin.
An octopus, flying fish, a parrot,
Anything you want.
A big tank of fish would do me
Anything at all from the sea.
I have nothing else but pets
I never get cold
I'm always warm.

Molly Kerrigan (9)
St Joseph's Convent School, Wanstead

HOME - THE BEST PLACE I COULD BE IS . . .

Home is the best place I could be,
With my mum, my dad, my sisters and me!
Home is a place where I can unwind,
Where I physically rest and also relax my mind.
Home is where I keep my baby Chou Chou,
Belle she's called, French for beautiful!
I could not live without my TV.
In EastEnders Mark's had HIV!
My sisters are five months and thirteen years old,
Our secrets together always unfold!
I sometimes call my older sister Yasmina,
(Yasmin she's called) and I don't like watching Tazmania!
Home is the best place I could be,
With my mum, my dad, my sisters, Yasmin and Soraya and . . .
Me!

Farah Omotosho (8)
St Joseph's Convent School, Wanstead

FRIENDS - FUNKY FRIENDS

Friends are fast
Friends are slow
Some are chubby
Some are grubby
Friends are nice
Friends are kind
Friends are cheeky
Friends are naughty
Friends are horse crazy
Friends are silly
Friends are funny
And that's the best about friends.

Sophia Plent (9)
St Joseph's Convent School, Wanstead

I'M DREAMING OF A LAND . . .

I'm dreaming of a land . . .
Where fairies flutter onto my hand
Where the flowers gently sway
Side by side, day by day
And in the spring the flowers grow
In the winter there is warm snow
As warm and light as sand
Guess what ? It doesn't freeze your hands!
The sun is always bright
And no one ever fights
There are lovely meadows and glorious hills
No one ever hurts or kills
There are kind people who live in bungalows
In this land there are no foes,
The skylarks happily fly the sky
There is healthy food instead of crisps and sweet pies
I wake up
My dream is gone, it's leaking out of my head like
Keeping water in a leaking cup.
I wish my dream could come true . . .
Not just for me, but also for you.

Porshia Athow (9)
St Joseph's Convent School, Wanstead

PETS - OUTSTANDING PETS

I love pets,
most are lovely and soft.
Pets are big, pets are small,
Some play in a loft.

I love dogs, cats and snakes
because they make a mess.
I would really like a pet
any sort yes, yes.

When I go to bed at night I dream
and dream about
lots of lovely pets
that's right.

Chantal Purser (9)
St Joseph's Convent School, Wanstead

THE CORAL PALACE

Diving down, down, *thump!*
I hit the seabed.
A rainbow of colour and a blast of adventure
Drills through my heart, just at a glance.
Shimmering light, pearly bubbles
glinting in the sunlight above.
A beautiful furl of coral encrusted
with barnacles and lovely shells.
Another world, beauty beyond image
Fit for an angel, but forgotten because
no one cares.
A palace made for a king or queen
long-lost, created from coral and silver coins.
I sit in a kelp chair and wait.
Suddenly deathlike spiders of ice crawl,
my veins, their passage.
Freezing cobwebs wrap me and try to
hide me away.
But I return to the surface,
regret still swirls through me because
now I'll never know whether everything was real.

Harriet Rose Halsey (9)
St Joseph's Convent School, Wanstead

Favourite Things - Yummy Yum Yum

Chocolate ice cream
Vanilla ice cream
Lovely things to eat
Chocolate sundae,
Marshmallows and sprinkles
Luscious things to eat.
Hundreds and thousands
Chocolate frog.
Savoury things to eat.
Crisps go crunch, sizzle and pop.
Yummy things to munch.
Chocolate bars, sticky caramel,
Yucky and mucky
Things to eat.
Lollipops you suck
And get in a muck.
(Scrumptious)
Chocolate fudge cake with fresh cream
Oh what a dream!
But one thing I love the most
Is . . . cheese on toast.

Claudia Zeppetella (9)
St Joseph's Convent School, Wanstead

My Friends Are Funny

My friends are funny
My friends are so nice
They're very nice
I think they're much better than spice.

My friends are loving
My friends are caring
Friends are always there
My friends are always nice to me
My friends will always care!

Tessa Kerslake (8)
St Joseph's Convent School, Wanstead

DEEP BLUE SEA

I was in my aqualung
I was going down
Down into the sea
To see what's down there.
There might be sharks
Or killer whales.
But it was my job to find out.
Splash as I got in
Here I go
Crowds watch me as I go
further and further
Until they can't see me.

As I went further into the sea
I saw an electric eel
Looking at me.
Rainbowfish and sea horses
Swam by me.
I even got to swim with the little dolphins.
A wreck came into view,
Could it be San Phillip?
I better take a closer look.

Ayesha Nicholls (9)
St Joseph's Convent School, Wanstead

EXPLORER BELOW THE SURFACE

The white ship faded from my sight,
As deeper and deeper I swam.
Fish fluttered by my side like butterflies,
A bush of seaweed dancing through the waves.
Such a beautiful sight,
A charmed way sway,
My breath bubbling,
Pops at the surface, I turn my head,
An octopus comes into sight.
With a spray of grey ink,
Like a grey horse's tail,
It's gone, hundreds of crabs burrowing through the sand
And hiding in their coral hideout.
The tail of a dolphin slips behind a rock,
Or did it?
My imagination runs wild.
Is that a treasure chest over there?
No, a rock.
My aqualung is getting heavy
I must swim to the surface.
I felt the cold breeze blowing my face,
The undersea life has disappeared.

Alicia Hempsted (9)
St Joseph's Convent School, Wanstead

FRIENDS - SPECIAL FRIENDS OF MINE

Friends are funny
Friends are chubby
Friends are kind
Friends like to find
Friends are cool

They sometimes rule
But I don't mind they're always kind
Friends are special
They sometimes are a mess
But they're the best.

Louise Lasfer (9)
St Joseph's Convent School, Wanstead

DOWN IN THE DEEP BLUE SEA

I leapt into the water
I swam down into the deep blue sea
My breath looked like pearls
A little fish came by
I went to see where he went
Then grey sand went everywhere
It was a crab, he almost bit me
I plunged off the ground with all my strength
There was a green bush I went to touch it but,

Millions of shrimps swam out to me.
There was a fish in the distance
It looked at me.
I swam to have a look, it was a rainbowfish
The rainbowfish was red, purple, blue all types of colours.
Behind the fish was a ship.
Then the water swayed from side to side
All of the fish swayed too.
There were some coins I picked some up.
Before I could go inside the ship I got too cold.
I swam up to the warm sun
I never forgot the deep blue sea.

Jessica Moruzzi (9)
St Joseph's Convent School, Wanstead

DEEP DOWN

I put on my wetsuit and snorkel
Ready to explore the deep blue sea,
Waiting to see the fishes and underwater life.

Deep down, deep down
Staring at fishes without a frown,
Whirling, twirling, round and round,
Trying not to touch the ground.

I dive in and start to swim,
Crabs and underwater life,
My dream to swim in the sea has come true.

Deep down, deep down
Staring at fishes without a frown,
Whirling, twirling round and round
Trying not to touch the ground.

I see an ancient shipwreck,
Deciding whether I should explore or not?
I go in and someone cries, 'Come in!'
I wonder what is going on?

Georgia Briggs (9)
St Joseph's Convent School, Wanstead

FRIENDS - WHAT I PLAY WITH MY FRIENDS

Friends are funny
Friends are fun
Sometimes they make me laugh and laugh
Friends cheer me up
And comfort me

Friends are joyful
Friends are mad
And once they pushed me in the mud
What a funny sight that was.
Friends are caring and loving.

Olivia Andani (8)
St Joseph's Convent School, Wanstead

MY ADVENTURE IN THE DEEP BLUE SEA

I put on my aqualung and dived into the deep blue sea,
So dark down there as dark as a cup of tea.
Oh no, I'm on the seabed,
Puffs of yellow smoke appear,
As crabs disappear.
Oh I wonder what's under that
cobweb of seaweed,
I must find out,
I feel bitter cold,
But I'm not scared.
Picking up a strand of seaweed,
And suddenly a shrimp whirlwind blows by.
I decide not to go on
There could be anything under there.
I swim to the top,
The beach again.
Normal life,
My world.

Faith Robins (9)
St Joseph's Convent School, Wanstead

TAKEN BY THE PIED PIPER

I was skipping along to the wonderful tune
The piper was playing to me,
It sounded so sweet so I lifted my feet
And ran along with him.

All the girls and boys with their cuddly toys
Were listening to that beautiful noise,
Then they all got a fright as they saw in the moonlight
The clashing waves just a few steps ahead.

But the piper turned
And led us to a cave
I wasn't afraid
Because I knew it would be something good.

With a *bang* and a *whizz* a crack opened
And all I could hear was
The pattering of little feet clattering
Trying to get in.

But inside was dreary and we were all very weary
From dancing so far, it was also quite damp
So I got my lamp and went over to the piper.

I told him I'd get the money
And he said to do it in a hurry
Before he changes his mind.

So I brought back the money
Once more he opened up the crack
And we all went through.

Now every Saturday evening
All the town comes down to the hall
And we listen to the
Delightful music that only the piper can play.

Niamh Sheehy (9)
St Joseph's Convent School, Wanstead

MY FIRST CLOSE LOOK AT THE SEA

I took a deep breath
And down I dive,
Into the secrets of the sea,
I look around the deep blue water,
Some bushes begin to falter.
Shrimps flying around,
Like little birds flying down.

The fishes just all swam away,
They were trying to hide from me!
Soon I see, a little baby crab,
Who disappears in a wisp of sand,
Like lots of yellow smoke.

Deep and deeper I go,
Till I stop at the sand.
I see my shimmering golden breath,
That almost looks like pearls.
As I swim and swim, I suddenly see,
A golden twinkle.
So I go as fast as I can
Tearing all the slimy seaweed.

I gasp as the sea reveals to me,
Lots of colourful starfish scuttling away.
Suddenly I can bear no more,
I need some air,
I don't want to suffocate!
I pulled myself back to the world,
Where I will always be.

I ran down to the crowds,
And thought, *this is where I belong!*

Pascale Bourquin (9)
St Joseph's Convent School, Wanstead

THE DEEP BLUE SEA

On goes my aqualung
I plunge in the water
Go deep, deep, deep down
Imagining what I'll see.
Some gold, oh a shark!
With all different things
What will I find,
Gold, money, cahoot, who knows?
Wow look at all these things
Fish like angelfish, oyster tiger etc.
Crabs, seaweed, wow!
Oh my gosh look at that treasure chest.
There might be some gold!
I go to the treasure chest and open the box.
Look at all that gold, if only I had a bag to put it all in.
Ahh who's behind me, I better go back to land
What an amazing trip
I should go again.

Tumi Unuefa (10)
St Joseph's Convent School, Wanstead

FANTASTIC FRIENDS

My friends are funny
My friends are nice
Like sugar and spice.

They are very kind
I could squeeze them tight!

They are caring and loving to me!

Harriet Blackshaw (9)
St Joseph's Convent School, Wanstead

ABDUCTED BY THE PIED PIPER

I skipped along,
To a song,
The Pied Piper played.
I was in a trance,
And I didn't glance,
To where he was leading me.
The mayor was standing straight,
In his suit,
While the Pied Piper
Played his flute.
The Pied Piper led us away,
Into a cave for the whole day.
The boy came with everyone,
And took us home again.
The mayor paid the money,
And everyone was jolly.
The Pied Piper went away,
And left us all alone again.

Sophie Radford (9)
St Joseph's Convent School, Wanstead

MY FRIENDS

Friends make you laugh,
Friends are funny,
Friends always let you play with them,
Friends are kind,
Friends are nice.

Friends always care for you,
Friends are special.

Sarah Hart (8)
St Joseph's Convent School, Wanstead

ABDUCTED BY THE PIED PIPER

I was woken by a man playing his flute
I ran downstairs and opened the door
I ran out with my friend Sally
We got kidnapped and
We went to a cave
We screamed and screamed
My mum and dad heard
They ran downstairs
But we had gone
He led us to a cave
It was spooky and dark.

When we were asleep
The piper went
I woke up for a glass of water
And I remembered where I was
In a cave
Then I realised the Pied Piper had gone
I found a digger and I started digging
David woke up and he helped, we shouted, we did it.
I woke everyone up and we all got out
And we all ran home.
We hugged our mums and dads
We were all so hungry
We all had some food
And went to bed.

Elizabeth Delima (10)
St Joseph's Convent School, Wanstead

THE DIVER'S TRIP

I dipped and I dived to the new enchanted world,
Where the fish and the sea horses lay
with coral moving side to side going backwards
and forth.

On and on I take and I steal
taking coins I feel wealthy now.
No one knows the secret except me.
The water felt old, dark and mysterious and scary.

Rachel Bonsu (10)
St Joseph's Convent School, Wanstead

I WAS TAKEN AWAY

I was singing, clapping and dancing away
Feet tapping, shoes clattering, shouting, 'Hooray.'
Little boys and girls,
Pearly teeth,
Golden curls,
Standing by the riverside.
Turned to a cave,
We all got in,
The music stopped.
Scared by the darkness.
We were stuck in a cave,
What shall we do?
The crippled boy,
Watched us get in.
He was so far,
He was left out.
He ran home, he started to shout
'Where are they?'
Our parents called in despair.
We heard them they were standing right there.
We were set free.
'Pied Piper, Pied Piper
I was set free,
What a silly man he was,
To try and capture all of us!'

Jasyme Robinson-Martin (9)
St Joseph's Convent School, Wanstead

FANTASY LANDS - CHOCOLATE WORLD

My fantasy land would be . . .
Chocolate lanes and sweets hanging from trees,
Candyfloss clouds and pink flowers everywhere.
Shops with clothes for everyone.
It would be so much fun.
Money would be made from beautiful chocolate.
All they would sell at the supermarket is chocolate and sweets.
The chocolate smell would fill the air.
My fantasy land would be made of chocolate and sweets
you could eat every day.
In the summer the sun would shine
and in the winter it would snow glitter.
That would be my fantasy land.

Martha Wilkinson (8)
St Joseph's Convent School, Wanstead

MUD FULL OF FUN

My fantasy land would be
Well you'll have to wait and see.

A big rainforest full of mud
Mud like chocolate
Full of fun
Quick, a snake, run, run, run!
Mud like chocolate
Full of fun.

Olivia Smart (9)
St Joseph's Convent School, Wanstead

MY FAVOURITE FRIENDS

There are curly-haired friends,
There are straight-haired friends,
There are short-haired friends,
And wavy-haired friends.
Friends that tell the truth and friends that tell lies
And friends that like to be spies.
There can be friends who like lots and lots of colours,
And friends who like to paint butterflies.
They can be nice and clever, some can be amazing and as light
as a feather, but everybody is a friend to me.
My sister, my brother and the rest of my family.

Akua Owusu-Ansah (9)
St Joseph's Convent School, Wanstead

FRIENDS - MY AMAZING FRIENDS

My friends are funny
My friends make me glad
My friends make me happy
When they hold my hand.

My friends are loving
My friends are caring
But sometimes they lie
That makes me cry.

That is why they are special to me.

Georgia Downes (9)
St Joseph's Convent School, Wanstead

HIDDEN DEPTHS

Way, way down in the depths of the sea,
I steal along.
Watching the bushes,
Wave to their song.
A sudden movement and a tornado of shrimps,
Circle all around me.
Angel and clownfish swoosh their fins,
In the freezing cold water.

Further on still I go,
With my aqualung.
Look! There goes a crab,
In a puff of golden dust.
An eel swims up to a pearl necklace,
I realise it's my breath!
I wonder what that cave hides?
Pirates treasure, silver and gold
Which look like sparkling chocolate wrappers.
Or cannons rusted with crusted barnacles
Like burnt toast.
But I shall never know.
Because right then blue hands,
Came up from the deep.
Starting to squeeze my neck.
Panic is sucking out all of my breath.
I swim up to the surface,
Before it is too late.
The warm air tickles my neck,
As I swim back to the fortissimo beach.
My world.
This is where I belong.

Louise Cottle (10)
St Joseph's Convent School, Wanstead

THE NON-ORDINARY WORLD

As I put on my aqualung
And plunged into the underworld
To see all the creatures
Creatures that no one else
Had ever seen before
In the underworld
It was deep and dark
But I could still see
As I swam around and around
I stopped, someone or something
Was making a noise
I felt my hand
Something was clasping it so tight
So tight my hand couldn't breathe
I looked, it was a crab!
A tiny little rosy red crab
How could I be afraid of that?
And just then at the corner of my eye
I saw something twinkle
Something so bright
It nearly blinded me
I swam to where I saw the twinkle
All there was, was seaweed
But as I dragged it
I found a treasure chest
I opened it, with a hairpin
Wow! I was amazed
There were gold coins everywhere
But as I got cold I had to go
Back to the ordinary world.

Christine Stokes (9)
St Joseph's Convent School, Wanstead

EXPLORING UNDERWATER

As I dived into the deep blue sea
Change of scene was taking place
Fishes swimming around my knee
Shades of blue darted in my eyes.

Shiny gold coins lay
As smoke of sand went away
I thought the seaweed was like spiders
Creatures still coming out the blue.

A crab was perched on a rock
I was getting cold, my fingers were numb
Fishes as colourful as my rainbow socks
I glided off the seabed.
Now I could hear familiar sounds of the human world.

Nicola Johnson (10)
St Joseph's Convent School, Wanstead

THE LAND IN MY HEAD - FANTASY LANDS

I wish there was a place where I could go,
All through the day, the wind would blow.
And in the springtime, flowers would grow,
Oh what a sight they'll be when they are on show.
The bees will buzz in the trees,
Making honey for you and me.
And my world's location is in my mind.
Oh, but I wish it could be real.
But it's only in my head.

Clare Davis (8)
St Joseph's Convent School, Wanstead

IN THE HOTEL

I pack my suitcase,
Oh do hurry up I say to myself,
Hop on the plane,
And off I go,
I arrive at a big hotel,
Creamy white,
All of a sudden I am finding
Myself dancing all the way
Up winding staircases.
I fling my bedroom door open and enter,
It seems like I am in Heaven.
Holidays, holidays,
There's nowhere better than
Holidays.

Isabelle Innes-Taylor (8)
St Joseph's Convent School, Wanstead

FRIENDS - FABULOUS FRIENDS

Friends are special,
Friends are helpful,
They always care for you
And you always care for them,
They give you gifts,
They please you,
You please them,
Friends are joyful,
Friends are playful.

Jessica Lebon (8)
St Joseph's Convent School, Wanstead

MY ADVENTURE IN THE SEA

My adventure in the sea,
Was as good as it could be,
When I jumped in the water,
All the fish swam away from me.

I found an old ship,
With its canons rusted,
And when I went inside,
All the pipes were busted.

I thought the adventure was good,
I thought it was great,
But there was one part of the adventure,
I started to hate.

Someone started holding me,
Up and up I went,
Then I realised my adventure in the sea,
Was coming to an end.

When I looked down at the seabed,
I saw puffs of sand,
Then I saw the crabs,
And thought they were very grand.

I swam back to the beach,
And heard the noisy crowds
And as I got faster,
Everything got loud.

Charlotte Crawford (9)
St Joseph's Convent School, Wanstead

Diving Experience

As I get my wet suit on
And oxygen mask,
Now I start my big experience
Deep below the sea.
I see angelfish
swimming away from me.

As I get deeper down
I see barnacles too and seaweed,
Swifting in the sand.
It couldn't be, it must be,
A wreck!
I swim away slowly,
In fear of skeletons.

As I touch a bush,
That blows up into a fish explosion
Beautiful colourful fish.
I see pearls next to me,
I touch them and they burst
It's my breath.

I see a dolphin
He swims under me,
Leading me to the surface
And then it's swimming away to my regret.
I feel cold and desperate
As I swim to the boat
And I had a hot chocolate.

Katherine Dadswell (9)
St Joseph's Convent School, Wanstead

DOWN IN THE SEA

Scuba-diving in I swam right down
Seeing fishes on my way
Landing on my feet
With a great big crush.
Yellow and gold smoke puffing on my face
Scaring the fishes
How cruel I am.

Swimming right down
I saw seaweed waving side to side
All in different types of green
Fishes all different too.

I saw a shell
And picked it up
I saw a crab
Hiding away
Thinking I would take it away.

I went deeper down
It was dark and cold
Seeing a dolphin
I jumped on its back
Giving me a ride
Back to the shore again
Looking at the world
I said, back to the old place again.

Thanupriya Sureshkumar (10)
St Joseph's Convent School, Wanstead

DOWN UNDER

I was all set to go,
Then something hit me
I couldn't find my oxygen tank
But it was right on my back.
I dived into the sea
All I could see was different fish in my face.
I saw a knobbly rock with things on it,
I went to see what it was,
I found out it was a pirate chest.
I opened it and it was gold treasure
It was starting to get cold, I swam up
To my ordinary home.

Hannah Sullivan (9)
St Joseph's Convent School, Wanstead

DIVING DOWN UNDER IN THE DEEP BLUE SEA

I was swimming deeper and deeper
I got to the bottom.
Looking back up the water so high up above me.
There were fish and crabs swimming by me.
It's dark under here like I was sitting in the dark.
I feel like a fish swimming around in the deep blue sea.
It's getting late, I should go home.
As I swam back, I said in my head
I had fun in the deep blue sea.

Louisa Grieve (10)
St Joseph's Convent School, Wanstead

FRUIT THE NUTCASE

There was a girl called Fruit the Nutcase,
Who never knew what she could do,
Who never knew what she could say,
Could not make sense in anyway.

So she asked her dad,
'Didn't he, Dad, do this . . . ?'
'Of course not.'

My grin was so wide
My grin was so wide that it connected to
the other side.

So she told her sister Summer,
'Sarha,' *sob*, 'said something silly, Summer.'
'Really, what did she say?'

My grin so wide,
My grin was so wide it was a grin I
couldn't hide.

There was a girl called Fruit the Nutcase,
who never knew what she could do until she knew.

Catherine Oyinlola (10)
Salisbury Primary School

ALL ABOUT HARRY

Some dogs are little
some dogs are fluffy
my name is Harry.
I'm big and I'm scruffy.

I don't need dog food,
I don't want a bone,
Just lots of love
please take me home.

Rebecca Lewis (10)
Salisbury Primary School

THE FANTASY SICK DRAGON

'What can I do?' Fantasy dragon cried,
'Although I've really tried,
It doesn't matter how hard I blow,
I cannot get my fire to go!'

'Open your mouth,' his mother said.
'It's no wonder your throat's not red,
Your scales are cold, you must be ill,
I think you must have caught a chill.'

The doctor came. He looked and said,
'You need a day or two in bed.
Your temperature's down, that's why,
your fire's gone out and your throat's dry.'

'Just drink these petrols, chew these nails,
They will help you to warm your scales.
Just take it easy, watch TV, you'll soon be well
again, you'll see.'

Fantasy dragon did as he was told, and soon
his scales stopped feeling cold.
He sneezed some sparks, his face glowed bright
And soon he felt, well again.

Musleh Uddin (11)
Salisbury Primary School

The Pen

The pen that told the truth,
Was inside the washing machine,
When it came out an hour later
It was soaking wet,
Days passed and the pen lay
There under the bed thinking
That it couldn't write anymore,
One day in the morning,
It was shining and it was really hot,
The pen wrote:
*How comes nobody needs me
and leaves me here lonely, alone?*
And much later it was another pen,
An undistinguished pen that hadn't
proved itself, that falsely wrote:
*Darkness gathers in the branches.
Stay inside and keep still . . .*

Albulena Meha (10)
Salisbury Primary School

Best Friend

We met up in the playground
then I went round for tea.
That's how the friendship started
for my best friend and me.

Sometimes we have a punch about,
Sometimes we play hockey,
also sit down and have a chat,
that's my best friend and me.

I've got lots of other friends,
like Zain, Rui and Musti,
but this one's something special,
my best friend and me.

Kulshan Bhakar (10)
Salisbury Primary School

GRANDAD

One day there was a boy
Who did as he was told
And when he grew up
Received a heart of gold.

He helped so many people
He helped the rich and poor
So everyone was pleasant
And never asked for more.

Then he died one day
There were so many tears
He was the one and only
One who really cared.

He didn't die of hurt
Or neither much of pain
So many went and stood for him
In the cold, wet rain.

So listen out you people
This tale is very true
Just do as you are told
Or it could just be you.

Isheetah Islam (11)
Salisbury Primary School

THE SMALL GHOSTIE

When it's late and it's dark
And everyone sleeps . . . shh shh shh,
Into our kitchen,
A small ghostie creeps . . . shh shh shh.

We hear knocking and raps
And then rattles and big bad taps.

Then he clatters and clangs,
And he batters and bangs.

And he whistles and yowls
And he screeches and howls . . .

And when I nod my head,
He falls out of bed.

So we pull up our covers over our heads,
And we block up our ears and
we stay in our beds!

Terri Gibbs (10)
Salisbury Primary School

HOBBIES

Satellite, satellite watching you every day
You are the way to end the day.
Up in the sky connecting to a TV
To make me more interested.
Instead of making me bored.
Satellite you are the one to make my day!

Masum Hussain (9)
Salisbury Primary School

MY LAND

The land of Hikabaloo,
I have imagined it,
You should too.

There is a creature called Tilly-Tear,
He is a very vicious bear.
There also lives a tiny creature,
That doesn't have that many features.
It is called a buballoo
that lives on the land of Hikabaloo.

There is an imaginary world in your brain
that sometimes can be a little pain.

There are many other creatures
such as the so called teachers.
They sometimes want to make me cry
when I need to say bye-bye.
And that is the end of my poem.

Aderinsola Dada (9)
Salisbury Primary School

SPACE

Space is really cool,
It's like a living jewel
I really can't be fooled
I'm going to go there now.

Zoom, zim, zap,
I'm following the map
Out in space
I think I'm in a race.

Samantha Hampton (11)
Salisbury Primary School

FANTASY LAND

My fantasy land,
Is a land where it's sunny,
No war, no hatred,
Just monkeys that are funny.
You see the waves gushing in the sky high above,
Making a beautiful rainbow.
Up, up high above
And now it is dark at night
And the stars are twinkling in the sky
The big, bright, white moon
Looking down on me below
Makes me want to fly, fly, fly.

Sheun Oshinbolu (10)
Salisbury Primary School

HOBBIES

My hobbies are tigers
I like lions too
And cobras
When fighting crocodiles.
I like birds also.
All kinds of animals I love.
I have another hobby, plants!
Some grow big like a tree,
Just because of me!

Bilal Anwar (10)
Salisbury Primary School

My Best Friend

My best friend is called Shereece,
Sometimes she gets up my knees
I don't know who we would turn to
if we broke up,
but I do know one thing
and that thing is
we're both going to cry
with tears from our eyes.
Sometimes Shereece gets on my nerves,
and today she sat near the boys.

Candice Terrelonge (9)
Salisbury Primary School

Best Friend

My best friend is Lola
I wish she never left
Sometimes we have a row
But the next day we sort it out.
I have many other friends like
Candice, Natlyer, Mustfa and Aobtian
We walk home together like family,
friends and cousin, but one of my
favourite and best friend is Lola.

Edirin Idogun (9)
Salisbury Primary School

MISSING INDIA

My mum misses India,
She misses her seven animals,
Four chickens
And three cows.

My mum misses India
She misses the food she ate,
Sweet tasty mangoes
And delicious gulab jammun.

My mum misses India
She misses the smell of the juicy fruits
Growing on spiky palm trees
With smiles on their hot faces.

My mum misses India
She misses her education
Remembering her mosque and her school
Gives her sad emotion.

My mum misses India
She misses Gujerat
Where she lived with her in-laws
For almost fifteen years.

Fawzan Ismail (10)
Selwyn Primary School

IN INDIA

In India there are three seasons
Summer, winter and monsoon.

In India some people are poor
They live in small villages.

In India mosquitoes bite you
while you're sleeping.

In India you can see the Taj Mahal,
one of the Seven Wonders of the World.

When I was in India I climbed on a slide
And twisted my ankle.

When I was in India I thought to myself,
I am safer in England than I am here.

Fatima Patel (10)
Selwyn Primary School

A WALK IN THE PARK

I see scaffolding
Strong and hard
Smelling of oil
Clanking with the constant sound
Of builders' boots.

I see traffic lights
Standing cold and tall
Stopping the cars
As the little green man
Flashes and beeps.

I see a stone sculpture
Rocky and craggy
I would like to climb up it
And sit on top
Surveying the world.

Daniel Drakes (11)
Selwyn Primary School

CELEBRATING EID

I love the festival of Eid
Waking up early
On a fresh winter morning
Going to Mosque
To pray.

I love the festival of Eid
Waking up early
To see my new clothes
Clean and beautiful
Just waiting for me
To wear.

I love the festival of Eid
Coming back from Mosque
To see my family
Waiting to give me
Lots and lots
Of money
To spend.

Lukman Hasan (10)
Selwyn Primary School

DIWALI

I love the festival of Diwali
When the divas
Twinkle and shimmer
Like sunshine sparkling on a calm sea.

I love the festival of Diwali
When we light our fireworks
Which sparkle and glimmer
In the dark autumn sky.

I love the festival of Diwali
When we visit the temple
Remembering our god, Rama
When he overcame Ravana, the cruel demon king.

Chhaya Mistry (11)
Selwyn Primary School

THE FLOATING MAIDEN

I can see
A young dead maiden
Floating on the surface of the lake
Wearing a long, faded, grey dress.

I can see,
A young dead maiden,
Her long ginger hair touching the tip of the lake
And her face pale all around.

I can see,
Multicoloured flowers,
Drifting from the maiden's hand,
How colourful they look.

I can see,
A fallen tree with a little blossom,
A tiny robin, sitting on a branch,
Lonely and afraid.

I can see,
Long, spiky, green grass.
Fringing on the edge of the lake,
Staring at the floating maiden.

Leena Gunamal (10)
Selwyn Primary School

GOING FOR A WALK

I see a bin
Smooth and plastic
Full up to the brim
With the odour of a skunk.
It says, 'Empty me,
I'm getting too fat,'
And I walk by, feeling disgusted.

I see a sign on the road
Red, where it's rusted
Tasting of metal,
Bumpy and dirty
It says 'Look at me,
I'm full of graffiti,'
I stop and think,
No parking here.

I see a palm tree
Smelling of coconuts
Sweetly tasting
Coarse and rough
On its hairy brown trunk
Standing up straight
Like the stalk of a pineapple.

I hear the wind
Rushing and sighing
Trying to blow
The leaves off the tree
And I feel sad
That the tree will be lonely
Now that winter is coming again.

Manisha Gunamal (10)
Selwyn Primary School

MACBETH

When the witches said
You would be Thane of Cawdor
And later king of Scotland
How did you feel?

I felt excited
When the first promise came true
I knew I would be king
As I'd always wished to be.

When you had to go
Into the dark bedroom
And kill King Duncan
How did you feel?

I knew there'd be big trouble
If ever I got caught
But if I didn't kill him
I'd never be the king.

When you planned the murder
Your wife was strong
She helped you
Do you love her?

I know that she was selfish
When she urged me on to kill
But I love her
Because she made me king
And she's my queen.

Raheema Azam (11)
Selwyn Primary School

CHRISTMAS

I love the festival of Christmas
Sparkling decorations
Dangle down
From a tall, green, spiky tree.

I love the festival of Christmas
Everyone rushing
Like Olympic runners
Buying their presents in crowded shops.

I love the festival of Christmas
Laughing children
Come out early
To build a snowman
With soft, white, flaky snow.

Robinah Kironde (10)
Selwyn Primary School

SPIDER-MAN

Spider-Man, Spider-Man
friendly neighbourhood Spider-Man
spins a web any size,
catches thieves just like flies.
Look out, here comes Spider-Man.
You're my man, you're my man,
You're my Spider-Man
and you can do whatever a spider can.
Look out, here comes Spider-Man
Look out, here comes Spider-Man!

James Parmenter (10)
Seven Mills Primary School

DAVID BECKHAM

As fast as a bulldog
Protecting his young
He runs on the pitch
Spoiling the fun
By bursting the ball
With his razor-sharp teeth
He runs around the pitch
Laughing at me
The players run and run
To catch his feet
They fall over and say
'Will you help me catch that bulldog?'

Jamie Murch (9)
Seven Mills Primary School

UNTITLED

Smuggler, smuggler,
Stealing things
And trading with things they bring,
Creeping round the street
With their little feet
Hoping that soldiers don't meet
His name was Tim,
His hair did need a trim.
His top was black
Holding a big sack
He finished the stealing
And ran with feeling.

Maria Luu (10)
Seven Mills Primary School

MY TRUE FRIENDS

As my true friend, you have helped me when
I needed it most,
As I would do for you.
When I was down you cheered me up and
told me about the happy times,
As I would do for you.
When I was in a tight spot, you were there
to stand up for me,
As I would do for you.
When I need to rely on someone
I know who to go to.
I am so happy for the relationship we have,
I feel so lucky to have a friend like you,
A true friend is like your own flesh and blood.

Sharmila Haque (9)
Seven Mills Primary School

MY FAMILY

My family, three brothers, one sister
So nice and so bright,
When I think about my family
I think they are always right at all times
Don't go to my brother or look in the room
So dark and so black
I think that's a lesson to you all
Don't go near my family.

Shahina Begum (9)
Seven Mills Primary School

THE TIDE RISES, THE TIDE FALLS

The tide rises, the tide falls,
The twilight darkens, the curlew calls,
Along the sea's edge, sands, damp and brown
The traveller hastens towards the town
And the tide rises, the tide falls.

Darkness settles on roofs and walls,
But the sea, the sea in the darkness calls,
The little waves with their soft white hands
Efface the footprints in the sands
And the tide rises, the tide falls.

The morning breaks, the steeds are in their stalls,
Stamp and neigh as the hostler calls;
The day returns, but never more,
Returns the traveller to the shore
And the tide rises, the tide falls.

Tasnia Foyaze
Seven Mills Primary School

THE SNAKE AND THE RIVER

The snake is like the river
always wriggling, always hissing.
Water rushing like a rattlesnake
through the damp grass.
When water floods the snake is drinking blood.
When the snake swerves, the river swerves too.
The river is searching for the sea.
The snake is rushing for its *prey!*

Harry Davidson (9)
Seven Mills Primary School

THE SMUGGLER'S SONG

If you have a fright at midnight and hear children's feet,
Don't go staring at the cat and dogs
Or looking in the street,
Then don't ask no questions to people.
Stare at the wall dear, while the children go by!
Fifteen and twenty people,
Walking through the night,
Whisky for the parson,
Baccy for the clerk,
Dresses for a lady, notes for a spy,
Stare at the wall, dear, while the children go by!

Ella Scrutton (9)
Seven Mills Primary School

IF YOU WAKE

If you wake in the morning and hear shooting guns,
Don't go yanking back the blind or looking in the street,
Them that ask no questions, don't get told a lie
Watch the war my darling, the soldiers go by!
Five and twenty tanks
Rolling through the dark,
Heading for the army
Baccy for the soldier
Letters for a spy
And watch the war my darling, while the soldiers go by.

Mitchel Skeels (9)
Seven Mills Primary School

A SMUGGLER'S SONG

If ya look in da evening and 'ear da children play
Don't go ignoring dem or running down da street
Dem dat kidnaps da kids isn't told a lie,
Watch da window, my darling, while the animals go by.
Six and twenty lions hunting through da dark,
Lemonade for da person, gold for da clerk
Rings for a lady, cameras for a spy,
And watch da window, my darling, while da animals go by.

Flaheen Alam (9)
Seven Mills Primary School

THE RHINO'S SONG

If you wake and hear rhinos' feet,
Don't go out. Just stay in bed or watch the street,
Them that ask no questions isn't told a lie,
Watch the horns my darling while the rhinos go by,
Five and twenty rhinos trotting through the dark,
Blood for the rhinos,
Baccy for the clerk,
Laces for a lady, letters for a spy,
Watch the horns my darling while the rhinos go by!

Ikramul Hoque (9)
Seven Mills Primary School

FRIENDS

Friends are people who you would want every night and day,
They always listen to every word you say.
Our friends are caring, helpful and nice,
They help when you are in trouble without thinking twice.
Our friends help calm you down when you are mad,
They help make you happy when you are sad,
They say, 'What's the matter, come and play out.'
This is what friends are all about!

Louis Sleap (9)
Seven Mills Primary School

FRIENDS - HAIKU

My friend is like a
Strawberry on a tree, blows
While children go by.

Jodie Cox (9)
Seven Mills Primary School

JERRY HALL

Jerry Hall is so small,
Rats can eat him, hat and all,
When he goes to bed,
He snuggles his friend called Fred,
Jerry Hall is so small,
Rats can eat him, hat and all.

Nahid Hoque (9)
Seven Mills Primary School

SCARED

Thunder is crashing outside
Perhaps I should go to bed
Hour upon hour comes and goes
What shall I do to forget it?
Perhaps tomorrow will be nice and sunny
Thunder starts to disappear
Rain turns to sunshine
I am not really scared
I will go to bed now.

Nima Begum (10)
Seven Mills Primary School

OUR WAY TO THE MAGIC LAND

When I opened my eyes
I saw I was in a beautiful green world.

I can see the green water next to me
I can see lots of trees around me with a blanket on me.
I can hear the sound of a cat and the sound of a dog.
I can hear a snake coming towards me.
I feel I am dying in this place.
I feel I am going to be eaten.

I can hear a girl crying.

I can see all of the island.
I can see the sun going down.
I can't go home again.

Marjana Chowdhury (8)
Shapla Primary School

JOURNEY TO AN IMAGINARY LAND

As I opened my eyes
I found myself on top of the high mountain
and a gigantic building was around me.

I could see the reflection of the building
and a sun on the still water.

I could see a dark sky and a bright blue sky
at the top of the buildings and
landscape where the sea met the sky.

I could hear a woodpecker making a sound
like a drilling noise, making a place to hide himself.

I could hear the sound of splashing water and
the waves crashing into the rocks.

I felt cool and hungry and I felt lonely
and on my own.

I was so sad but then I saw the beautiful sun
and I was happy to be alive.

Abidur Rahman (8)
Shapla Primary School

JOURNEY TO AN IMAGINARY LAND

As I open my eyes I find myself
in a dark night with stars shining bright.

I can see the birds flying
and all the stars are coming towards me.

I can see the moon
shining bright and beautifully like a brand new silver coin.

I can hear the seagulls making noises from far, far away
and I can hear the clouds moving gently.

I can hear the birds singing beautifully
and I think that I also have a sweet voice like a bird.

I feel that it is snowing
and I can feel that the trees are falling.

Farheen Begum (8)
Shapla Primary School

MY SPECIAL BOX
(Based on 'Magic Box' by Kit Wright)

In my box I will put . . .
A photo of the first-ever friend I made,
The wish that a shooting star can hear.

In my box I will put . . .
The rays from the sun and moon,
A never-ending story that no one can end.

Inside my box I will put . . .
A unicorn's wing
That is the colours of a rainbow sent from Heaven.

My box is made from the dazzling dreams I have had,
The gentle touch of my skin.
My box is made from the sun and moon.

I will hide my box way up high in Heaven
So the man in the moon can get it and open it,
Then one day all the things in my box
Will float back down to Earth.

Najmen Akhter (9)
Shapla Primary School

PAINT ME

Paint me as black as space
So I can see all the stars and the sun
Paint me as green as leaves
So that I can see from above the sky
Paint me as blue as the ocean
So I can see the ocean whirl around
Paint me as yellow as a fierce lion
So I can show how fast I am
Paint me as white as an Egyptian mummy's bandages
So I can sleep in my coffin
Paint me as invisible as the wind
So I can blow everyone away.
Paint me as grey as a manatee
So I can roll in the muddy water
Paint me as red as a fire engine
So I can drive to the rescue
Paint me as grey as the pavement
So people can walk on me.
Paint me as gold as the Egyptian mummy's case.

Azizul Haque (8)
Shapla Primary School

MY DRAGON

I am a fierce dragon
I fly through the cloudy blue sky
I can transform into any creature
I have skin like a snake
I live in the blue shimmering ocean
I am the king of the world
I have a tail like a mermaid under the ocean

I have a powerful pearl in my mouth
I am the colours, jade and scarlet
I have hot, fiery breath
I sing very loudly so everybody can hear me
I have gold sharp teeth
I have a scarlet tongue with gold stripes
I am a fierce dragon, so beware of me!

Sharmin Shanaz (9)
Shapla Primary School

MORNING

Morning comes
    With Dad moaning

Morning comes
    With alarm clock ringing

Morning comes
    With wind whooshing

Morning comes
    With cars vrooming

Morning comes
    With nephew screaming

Morning comes
    With brother poking

Morning comes
    To take me to school - I love the morning.

Nasir Uddin (9)
Shapla Primary School

DRAGON

I am a gigantic dragon
The lord of the water and the sky
Glittering through the glowing stars
Like a bird
I swim like a sea lion
I have a horn of a unicorn
My mate is the sun who burns everything
My friend is the moon who is frozen still looking for me
I am a dragon
Who never ever lets anyone touch my special pearl
I have a snake's body
I have a shark's growing fin
I have the tiger's shimmering teeth
I am powerful
And I have the beast's claws.

Nayem Ahmed (9)
Shapla Primary School

JOURNEY TO AN IMAGINARY LAND

As I opened my special eyes
I found myself.

I'm in a Monaco Hollywood 'summer' resort
I can see lots of lights in the buildings.
I can see lots of people.
I can hear a boat howling like a wolf.
I can hear lots of people screaming, shouting,
                    dancing and singing.
I feel lonely.
I wish my mum and dad were here.
But I'm still happy and well.

Faroqul Islam (8)
Shapla Primary School

Dragon

I am a mighty dragon.
I can fly faster than anything in the whole universe.
I breathe amber and gold fire.
When I am saving someone I use my thunder balls.
At night my unicorn horns shine like lightning
So people can see me.
I fill people's money boxes with golden coins.
My silky scales are turquoise and amber.
I have eyes like the sun and moon.
I have a head of a lion and a body of an anaconda.
Sometimes my body changes into a beast-like body.
My eyes are as red as blood.
The end of my tail is fire.

Mizan Rahman (9)
Shapla Primary School

Dragon

I am a mighty dragon,
I have glimmering wings,
I am friendly
When people are friendly to me,
I have a magic pearl in my mouth,
When I open my mouth the spring rain comes,
I have shimmering scales,
I can transform into really friendly animals like rabbits,
I can swim like a dolphin,
I am the colours, scarlet, jade and gold,
I am the ancestor of an emperor.

Shubey Begum (9)
Shapla Primary School

MORNING

Morning comes
    With the sun rising
Morning comes
    With the flowers growing
Morning comes
    With light shining
Morning comes
    With my mum calling
Morning comes
    With my brother crying
Morning comes
    With my shouting
Morning comes
    With my dad singing.
Morning comes
    With, 'I have to go to school.'
Boss-woman, morning.

Farhana Begum (9)
Shapla Primary School

THE SUN

The sun is a golden conker
Held by a giant.
The sun is a one pound coin
dropped on the light blue carpet.
The sun is a phoenix
flying all around.
The sun is a dazzling plate
dropped in water.

Sayeem Yaheya (8)
Shapla Primary School

MORNING

Morning comes
    With the sun singing
Morning comes
    With Mum shaking
Morning comes
    With the milk splashing
Morning comes
    With Coco Pops crunching
Morning comes
    With postman posting
Morning comes
    With flowers growing
Morning comes
    With baby laughing
Morning comes
    With people hiding
Morning comes to drag me out of bed
    Boss-woman, morning.

Farhana Lucky Rouf (9)
Shapla Primary School

DRAGON

I am a dragon.
I have a pearl in my mouth
Burning like fire.
I sleep in the misty mountains.
I can swim through the shining water.
I have dazzling scales and crimson fire.
I have a gold tail so I can swirl it around
In the misty mountains.

Junel Ali (9)
Shapla Primary School

JOURNEY TO AN IMAGINARY LANE

As I opened my eyes
I could see everything dry
And I could see green grass and a lake
There was ice on the ground.
I couldn't see the reflection of the clouds as they made shapes.
I could see the eagles flying by, singing.
I could hear the woodpecker making a hole so he
could hide himself and nobody would find him.
I could hear a bird calling to me to go and have a rest.
It felt so different because I was in a different land
and everything was new.
I felt hungry and sleepy and I wanted to sleep
and also eat but I couldn't open my eyes!

Abdul Azim (8)
Shapla Primary School

JOURNEY TO AN IMAGINARY LAND

As I opened my eyes
I found myself in a place that was dark like a forest.

I can see lots of trees and they are spooky.
I can see lots of flowers and there is a very strong smell
And I feel very tired.

I can hear the wind waving and the trees moving
I can hear birds flying away and water splashing in the river.

I feel like I must run away from the forest.

At last I am happy because I have run away.

Amena Ahmed (8)
Shapla Primary School

MY SPECIAL BOX
(Based on 'Magic Box' by Kit Wright)

In my box I will put . . .
Dug-up crystals from the garden.
I will put in my family's love and never let it out.
I will put in my treasure from the seaside.
I will put in my happy times.
I will put in magic dust from the end of the rainbow.

My box is made out of silver thread from a fairy's wand.
Stars from a wizard's wand.
Words from a witch's book.

I will hide my box in the misty night
Way up high on the lonely moon
So when I whistle it, it will throw out a ribbon
So I can climb it and sit peacefully on the moon.

Masuda Hoque (8)
Shapla Primary School

JOURNEY TO AN IMAGINARY LAND

As I open my eyes
I find myself in a forest
and nobody is here.

I can see sparkling eyes
I can see a lot of branches.
I can hear owls hooting in the field.

I can hear cats miaowing and foxes howling
in the night.

I feel happy but the cats are shocked.

Samad Hussain (7)
Shapla Primary School

MORNING

Morning comes
    With the sun shining
Morning comes
    With the birds whistling
Morning comes
    With cornflakes crunching
Morning comes
    With my mother shaking
Morning comes
    With alarms ringing
Morning comes
    With the milkman delivering
Morning comes
    With a 'push me off to school'
Boss-woman morning.

Shamima Begum (9)
Shapla Primary School

JOURNEY TO AN IMAGINARY LAND

As I opened my eyes
I found myself in grassland.

I can see lots of trees,
I can see grass all around me,
I can hear owls hooting,
I can hear bears growling,
I feel so sad by myself
But at last I am so happy because
I've found a house to be at rest.

Farzana Begum (8)
Shapla Primary School

MORNING

Morning comes
    With golden toast flying
Morning comes
    With my sleepy dad moaning
Morning comes
    With gentle birds humming
Morning comes
    With an alarm clock jingling
Morning comes
    With babies crying
Morning comes
    With windy weather blowing
Morning comes
    To get me out of bed
            Lovely-woman morning.

Mujibul Hoque Miah (8)
Shapla Primary School

DRAGON

I am a dragon.
I have a pearl in my mouth.
I have sharp horns.
I live in the shiny water.
I have fire in my mouth.
I have sharp teeth.
I have a colossal tail.
My body is like a snake.
My eyes are red.

Shourov Ahmed (8)
Shapla Primary School

DRAGON

I am a mighty fierce dragon
I can transform into any living creature
I am a golden dragon
I have got the body of a slithery snake
A tail like a lion
And legs like a fierce eagle
I've got scales like a fish
The lethal teeth of a tiger
The horns of a unicorn
I can breathe fire from my mouth
I'm the king of the sun
I get my fire from the sun
I've got whiskers from the beautiful sun
I am powerful
I can see through disguises
I sleep in a secret place.
I am a deadly dragon!

Tawhid Choudry (8)
Shapla Primary School

JOURNEY TO AN IMAGINARY LAND

As I opened my eyes
I found myself near a deserted castle
and nobody was there.

I can see water coming from the
sea and a castle.
I can hear the birds singing.

I feel very lonely.
But I can see the moon and light.

Sayma Begum (7)
Shapla Primary School

DRAGON

I am a dragon
I live in the misty clouds
I am a dragon
I have the antlers of a deer
The tongue from a lion
The body of a slimy snake
I have two pearls for eyes
I am a dragon
I can transform into any creature
I have the teeth of a vampire
I can dive in the splashing sea
I am a dragon
The most powerful
I am the king of the land
No one can take that away from me.

Nazia Begum (8)
Shapla Primary School

OPEN EYES

As I open my eyes
I see myself in a green valley
with tall, tall trees and evergreen bushes.
I can see the low branches of trees
are touching the black, black water
as if they are touching your heart
Far, far away I can also see a house
as if it's calling me just for a rest
and to think about me.
Why am I here?
From a distance I can see nothing
but green and brown leaves.

Hafsa Rahman (8)
Shapla Primary School

JOURNEY TO AN IMAGINARY WORLD

As I opened my eyes
I found myself in a dark, dark forest
I can see spooky trees and a scary fox
I can see a spooky castle
and the door is really disgusting
it's covered with spider webs
I can hear birds flying in the sky
and Mona, the vampire, is eating all the people.
I can hear screaming like a lion
I feel I am in a desert
but I am not in a desert
I am lonely.

Fatema Begum (8)
Shapla Primary School

DRAGON

I am the most helpful dragon in the universe
I don't kill people
I let people touch my pearl
I let people fly on my back across the world
I breathe fire on vicious people
I can transform
I can defeat bad dragons anytime
I can be very shiny without scales
I fly like a bird
I can fly through the clouds.

Shahid Mohammad (9)
Shapla Primary School

DRAGON

I am a legendary dragon
I am blazing and fierce
I sleep in the deep dark ocean
I have the eyes of a shark
I bring the spring rain
I have mighty wings to fly through the sky
I have the scales of a glimmering fish
I have the power of a phoenix
I can swim like a dolphin
I am as colourful as a rainbow
I have the thread of the sun and the moon
I am the lord of all the oceans.

Muntaha Wadud (8)
Shapla Primary School

DRAGON

I am a gentle dragon,
I sleep in the mysterious mountain,
I can transform into any living animal,
I have claws like a lion,
In spring I bring the rain,
I fly like a phoenix,
I've got breathing fire like the sunset,
I am an ancestor of an emperor,
I sing in the dazzling blue ocean,
I am king of the mountains.

Ataur Rahman
Shapla Primary School

MORNING

Morning comes
    With loud alarms ringing
Morning comes
    With a noisy bird flapping
Morning comes
    With stormy rain tapping
Morning comes
    With Mum talking
Morning comes
    With doors knocking
Morning comes
    With bathroom water splashing
Morning comes
    To shout me out of bed

This is a noisy, noisy morning!

Amrina Jahan (8)
Shapla Primary School

THE MOON

When the sun goes down and the moon comes up,
The moon is a light of Heaven
It is a white shining football
It is a beautiful shining meteorite from deep space
It is somebody's good luck charm
It is a soul of a spooky ghost
The moon is a medal of honour
The moon is God's creation.

Ibrahim Khalil (9)
Shapla Primary School

MORNING

Morning comes
    with brother dressing
Morning comes
    with TV watching
Morning comes
    with cars racing
Morning comes
    with bath water splashing
Morning comes
    with baby sister screaming
Morning comes
    with gentle birds humming
Morning comes
    to go to school.
I like the morning.

Abul Khaled (9)
Shapla Primary School

DRAGON

I am a dragon
I live in the sea
I fly in the sky
I am big and strong
I am green and gold
I have a pearl in my mouth
I have green eyes.

Jalal Uddin (8)
Shapla Primary School

MY SPECIAL BOX
(Based on 'Magic Box' by Kit Wright)

Inside my box I will put . . .
Drops of potions from the green-eyed wizard,
I will put lightning from the gloomy sky.

Inside my box I will put . . .
Evil witches' souls that turn you into snakes,
Pearls, the colours of silver and amber.

Inside my box I will put . . .
A newborn baby's first smile,
Silver threads from the moon.

In my special box I will put . . .
A secret note from a slimy alien,
The tears of a poor girl.

Inside my box I will put . . .
A multicoloured leaf that fell from Heaven,
My one and only grandmother's love.

My box is made from
A unicorn's horn, magical silk,
A red ruby.

I will put my box up in the sky,
Sitting on the moon
Until a shooting star will come
To take me to my special box
Inside my magic box.

Irina Sulltana Jahin (9)
Shapla Primary School

MORNING

Morning comes
    With Mum and Dad snoring *zzzzzzzzz!*
Morning comes
    With birds humming
Morning comes
    With cornflakes crunching
Morning comes
    With toaster popping
Morning comes
    With letters dropping
Morning comes
    With rain pouring
Morning comes
    With milkman jingling
Noisy milkman
Morning!

Farhana Kadir (9)
Shapla Primary School

THE SUN

The sun is a sunflower
Floating in the sky.
The sun is a golden conker
Ready to be cracked.
The sun is a yellow balloon
Ready to be popped.
The sun is a dragon's fire breath
That had been blown years ago.

Mohammed Ashraf Hussain Chowdhury (9)
Shapla Primary School

DRAGON

I am a dragon
I am the king of the world
I have a magical pearl in my mouth.
I have muscular wings so I can fly through the sky
No one can catch me

I am a dragon
I have fire in my mouth
My fire is amber and scarlet
I have scarlet scales on my body
The scales are smooth like a feather
I am a dragon
Beware of me!

Iqbal Hussain (9)
Shapla Primary School

DRAGON

I am a bold dragon
I am a terrible dragon
I can flame a mighty pearl
I can transform any animal
I have a gleaming pearl
I am a dangerous dragon
I can fly as fast as a cheetah
I have a wing of a large eagle that hunts
I have a body of slithery skin like an anaconda
I have the longest tail in the universe
I sing in the dark blue ocean
I have the colours of the scaly fish
I am the king of the clouds.

Aminul Islam (9)
Shapla Primary School

WHAT SISTERS ARE FOR

A sister is a friend, a sister is someone to look after,
they may scream sometimes but they are always your sister.
A sister may be a disaster,
but can be sorted out.
They may run faster,
but that doesn't matter because they are still your sister.
A sister may not dress nicely,
but they are still your sister.
They may have more money
which is really annoying
but they are still your sister!

Gemma Beswick (9)
Snaresbrook Primary School

CATS

Cats are cute and cuddly,
They make me feel warm and bubbly.
They are naughty but friendly
And always keep you company.

Sometimes they can be *very hungry,*
They often eat twice
And are very good at catching mice,
They never hunt in herds
But are well-known for stalking birds.

That's what a cat does when . . .
                              it's hungry!

Yasmeen Mukadam (9)
Snaresbrook Primary School

ALL ABOUT ME

My hair is as black as the night,
My skin is as brown as wood,
My eyes are as brown as dark chocolate,
My lips are as pink as a pink tulip!

My dad is as tall as a giraffe,
My mum is as small as a mouse,
My grandad is as old as time,
My grandma is funny and giggly!

My favourite subject is art,
My favourite teachers are Miss Foy and Miss Collier,
My favourite sweets are chocolates,
My favourite author is Roald Dahl!

I love to skip and run and swim,
I love to eat spaghetti,
I love to go to school,
Where I'm really cool!

Archanna Gunasekaram (9)
Snaresbrook Primary School

ALL ABOUT ME

I'm a girl with bright brown hair
Although my eyes are very fair
I have a sister whose name is Lily
And a friend whose name is Dilly.

I'm quite short and eight years old
And I always do as I'm told
I like to play games which make me happy
But I don't like changing my sister's nappy.

I like to play music on the recorder
And I've been on holiday to the Italian border
My favourite fruit is strawberries
And my favourite shop is Sainsbury's.

Lydia Clark (8)
Snaresbrook Primary School

AT THE FUNFAIR

I hear people scream
as they go upside down
I hear the Terminator
twisting round and around.

I see the big wheel
go up and down
I see a spooky ghost train
and a very funny clown.

I smell the salty chips
and the spicy sauce
I smell sweet candyfloss
and a very smelly horse.

I fiddle with the sweaty coins
as I glare at the rides
I hold onto the mats
as I go down the slides.

I taste the crunchy fish
and the salty chips
I taste the toffee apples
and spit out the pips!

Sehar Ishaq Khan (9)
Snaresbrook Primary School

PICKING THINGS

Jack picks Jon,
Jon picks Rose,
Someone picks me and I pick my nose . . .

But . . .
If I pick my nose
Who does my nose pick?

My nose must pick someone,
It's a picking game,
So why can't my nose pick?

It sounds so lame.

Matthew William Hill (8)
Snaresbrook Primary School

HAMSTERS

Hamsters are cute and cuddly.
Mine makes me feel all bubbly.

He sleeps in a ball and is very small.
He nibbles his food and is always in a good mood.

But I don't like the smell in his cage.
My hamster is a very good age!

Shauna Jane Butler (8)
Snaresbrook Primary School

THE POLAR KANGAROO

Have you heard of the polar kangaroo?
He lives in a pink igloo
When he jumps the ice breaks
And he loves to make cakes!

The polar kangaroo asked, 'Why did the cow say moo?'
And the cockerel said, *'Cock-a-doodle-doo'*
But the only answer he got was . . .
'Moo, moo, moo, cock-a-doodle-doo!'

Harriet Clarke (8)
Snaresbrook Primary School

STARLAND

In Starland . . .
There are castles floating in the air,
The princess is brushing her long golden hair,
Unicorns with silver horns,
The sunrise is pink as the day dawns,
The smell in the air,
The land is so fair.
I sit on the soft sand
In my dreams in Starland!

Pippa Wiskin (8)
Snaresbrook Primary School

WAR

The thump of the army's marching feet.
The screaming of children trying to find their parents.
The red grass of blood on the battlefield.
The death of men and women.
The crash when planes explode.
The blast of weapons when fired.
Destruction of buildings.
Doctors and nurses holding back death.
Look to peace after war!

Alexander McKie (9)
Snaresbrook Primary School

A Corrupt World

One misty, tranquil night,
When the only noise to be heard was the endless legions of waves
Hitting the jagged rocks,
The lady came out of the sea,
Eyes like ripples on a vast pool,
Small, gentle and palest blue,
She gazed down on the dry, barren wasteland,
So much had changed since she last escaped her subterranean prison,
No longer was it heavenly and divine,
The wind whipped up a frenzy,
With pain, she realised her freedom was not meant to be,
The prisoner re-entered her prison.

William Brown (9)
Snaresbrook Primary School

Summer And Winter

Summer is sweet,
Winter is dull,
Summer is wonderful,
And winter is cold.

Winter is numbing,
Summer is hot,
Winter is frosty
And summer is my personal
                        favourite!

Rebecca Adams (8)
Snaresbrook Primary School

THE SEA

How I love the sea
It's just great for me,

I saw a great big squid,
To my surprise it hid,

Next we saw a shark,
Which happened to hide in the dark,

We caught a fish,
Which swam to our dish,

What a lovely day we had,
Luckily it was not sad.

Alice Roe & Rhys Jones (7)
Wanstead Church Primary School

GOOD FRIENDS

Anna, popular, leader, hip, cool.
Anna.
Amy, understanding, motherly, listener.
Amy.
Caitie, bouncy, fun, enjoyable, laughable.
Caitie.
Sarah, imaginative, there when you need her.
Sarah.
Megan, one friend, true friend, best friend.
Megan.
Me, me, me, me
Me.

Imogen Steinberg (11)
Wanstead Church Primary School

FLOWERS

Tulips, daffodils, roses
Lavender, bluebells and posies.

Flowers are neat,
They smell so sweet.

Lavender, daffodils, posies,
Tulips, bluebells and roses.

Chrysanthemums, daisies, buttercups,
Dandelions, lilies, snowdrops.

Flowers sometimes make you sneeze
With pollen blowing in the breeze.

Dandelions, daisies, snowdrops,
Chrysanthemums, lilies, buttercups.

Ellen Phillipson (8)
Wanstead Church Primary School

THE WAVES

Calm waves, rough waves,
Quiet or loud waves,
Waves that are big waves,
Waves that are small,
Waves that are very loud on the shore,
Waves that are green,
Waves that are blue.
These are the waves I have seen.

Elise Woolnough (8)
Wanstead Church Primary School

BEST FRIENDS

B is for *beautiful* and the best,
E is for *elegant* and the rest,
S is for *sugar* and sweet,
T is for *tasty* friendship we meet.

F is *forever* love and care,
R is for *rubbish* you talk about and your dares,
I is for *ignorant* things you do,
E is for *enjoyment,* you don't have a clue,
N is for *niceness* you can share,
D is for *dates* you fight over, you need some air!

Rosie-May Mary Parker (10)
Wanstead Church Primary School

FEBRUARY

F ebruary is fun,
E motional things happen like:
B irthdays and parties,
R hys and I have our birthday on the 18th of February.
U nhappy children turn happy at once
A re you happy?
R eady to have fun?
Y es, I am!

Justin Hung & Carys Jones (7)
Wanstead Church Primary School

SWEETS

Sweets are great
Some are sticky
Some are hard.
Little lollipops
Chewy caramel
Sweets are fun
For everyone.
It's time for sweets
Hooray!
Ticklish liquorice treats
Are lots of fun
Some are long
Some are short
Some are curly.
I wish it would rain sweets.
They are yummy
They tickle your tummy
There are lots of sorts
They rule!

Ellen Hepworth (9)
Wanstead Church Primary School

THE DRAGON CAME TO TOWN

D id you see the dragon
R unning and raging down the street?
A ll around him people stared,
G iggling at his feet.
O n he went from town to town, causing laughter all around.
N ever did we see such a colourful sight!

James Hall (7) & Nadine Baker (8)
Wanstead Church Primary School

Describing My Cat

Fluffy fur,
quiet purr,
light treading paws,
razor blade claws,
wet nose,
has a doze,
cat's food,
changes its mood,
sleeps by the fire,
to its heart's desire.
Plays with the wool,
tosses the bouncy ball,
wants affection,
gets your attention,
its big green eyes,
open very wide,
silky whiskers.
That's my cat.

Priscilla Hampton (10)
Wanstead Church Primary School

Flowers

Flowers are blue
Flowers are green
Flowers are pink
Flowers are cream

Flowers blooming
Flowers looming.

Rebecca Fanning (8)
Wanstead Church Primary School

FOOTPRINTS IN THE SNOW

Snow,
White, deep snow.
Footprint,
Black, large footprint.
Here,
There,
Left,
Right,
In front,
Behind,
Never-ending,
Ever going,
Footprints in the snow!

Caitriona Elizabeth Ferguson (11)
Wanstead Church Primary School

RATS

Rats in the station
Rats in the sewers
Rats in the street and in the forest
But rats have to be careful
For they are a meal for a cat
Some carry diseases
But some are pets
Some go up the toilets
Some go in the dustbins
Lots of people are terrified of *rats!*

Christopher Gardner (9)
Wanstead Church Primary School

HAIR

Brown hair,
Blond hair
Ginger hair
Curly hair
Straight hair
F u z z y hair
Long hair
Short hair
Resting on your hip hair
We all like different,
Maybe *messy*
Maybe neat!

Chloe Buck (8)
Wanstead Church Primary School

FOOTY

Boot it high
and boot it higher.
Boot it right in the goal,
see it whizzing past the keeper,
see it returned back to you.
Punch it out,
kick it out,
when you are the keeper,
if you let one in,
don't get upset,
you can still win.

Madeleine Greene (9)
Wanstead Church Primary School

MY FAMILY

My family,
My group,
My gang,
My support,
My herd,
My bundle,
My flock,
My cluster,
My rock,
My school,
My pack,
My pride,
My club,
My lot,
My colony,
My litter,
My cover,
My shoal,
My host,
My cloud,
My joy,
My crowd,
And until further notice,
My family!

Grace Tierney (11)
Wanstead Church Primary School

WEATHER

Weather is hot,
Weather is cold,
Weather is strong,
Weather is bold.

Tornadoes, monsoons, thunder and lightning.
Weather can be wet,
Weather can be dry,
Weather can be quite frightening.

Grace Twinn (9)
Wanstead Church Primary School

SCHOOL FOOTBALL

It's rough, it's tough,
It's slow, it's fast,
It's school football.

It's two-nil,
It's England versus Brazil,
It's school football.

It's blood and plasters,
Goals and disasters,
It's school football.

The window goes *crash!*
'Down the line, *bash!*'
It's school football.

Daniel Mannion (11)
Wanstead Church Primary School

BUBBLES

Bubbles are big, bubbles are blue,
Bubbles are round, bubbles are see-through
They fly so high, they reach the sky,
They flow like my dreams, then fade and die.

Joe Rees (9)
Wanstead Church Primary School

SAD

When I'm feeling sad,
Things look rather bad,
I don't want to paint,
And I don't want to go to the Tate,
I'm sorry I called you names,
But I think I feel the same.

I'm sorry I destroyed it,
But I think I did a bit,
My head is in a twist,
So I don't really care,
So I think I feel rather bad
Today.

Amy Iona Fanning (11)
Wanstead Church Primary School

WHAT HAS MISS SMITH GOT IN HER HOUSE?

Has she got cats?
Has she got dogs?
Has she got hamsters?
Has she got frogs?

Has she got a mouse in her handbag?
Or a tiger in her kitchen?
Or a rabbit in her bathtub?
Or even a hedgehog in her bed?

Whatever she's got in her house,
I bet it's one of these.

Aimee Evans (10)
Wanstead Church Primary School

YESTERDAY

If I could have one wish,
I would go back to yesterday
Why did I shout?
Why did I run?
What am I doing on the streets?

If I could have another wish,
I would have stopped myself,
Why did I steal that thing?
Why did I think I would get away?
Will I ever get out of this police cell?

Madeleine Simpson (10)
Wanstead Church Primary School

CLASS? WHAT?

A brick holding back the door,
Teacher's desk a state,
Pupils act like monkeys in caves,
And students creeping in late,
Girls sniggering on the back row
Boys' stickers under the table,
A zoo this is, a clue this is,

Class 6 this is!

Anna McGetrick (11)
Wanstead Church Primary School

HOBBIES

In the world we have lots of hobbies.
Swimming is a nice time to get out
Writing, we can write stories, poems, lots of things
These are only a couple, so I'll tell you some more,
Sport, to keep fit.
Making things, get creative!
Cooking, 'I'm hungry.'
There are many more that I can't tell you now,
So choose yours very carefully!

Charlotte Springett (9)
Wanstead Church Primary School

FOREST FIRE

The flames of the fire burning brightly
The firemen running fairly lightly
The trees of the forest you can see
The animals and the bumblebee
Perish and watch to see
Their homes burnt down!

Christopher Churchett (9)
Wanstead Church Primary School

MIXED FEELINGS

Right now I feel angry with my friends.
Right now I am happy with my work.
Right now I feel sad inside.
Right now I have mixed feelings.

Melissa Relfe (10)
Wanstead Church Primary School

FLOWERS

Flowers are pink
Flowers are blue
We know that they can be all different colours
The stem is so long, as long as a tail
It's green, oh so green, just like a leaf
As long as some grass
Flowers are pink
Flowers are blue
We like to smell flowers, oh they do smell quite nice.

Heather Yarwood (8)
Wanstead Church Primary School

MONSTERS

Monsters can be thick and hairy
Monsters can be big and scary.
They hide under beds
Live in caves.
Monsters can be thick and hairy
Monsters can be big and scary.

Nicholas Allen (7)
Wanstead Church Primary School

DINOSAURS

Tyrannosaurus, stegosaurus, triceratops too
put them all together, they make a dino group.
There are many, many more
I shall not name them now
but look, beware, the meat eaters are coming now.
Ahhhhh!

Georgia Surridge (8)
Wanstead Church Primary School

I Want This

I want this.
I want that.
You can't have this.
You can't have that.
That's unfair!
I don't care
So you can't have this
And you can't have that.

Bethany Walker (11)
Wanstead Church Primary School

Dumb!

Ting, tang, tong
That is wrong,
Splish, splash, splosh
Oh my gosh,
Nang, ning, nong
That's too long,
Oh no, you're stupid!

Paul Andrew Gardner (11)
Wanstead Church Primary School

The Sea

The sea crushes
Hear the noise
Intelligent animals
Singing softly
Intelligent animals
Appearing in the sea, *splash, splash, splash!*

Katie Alice McLean (8)
Wanstead Church Primary School

FOOTBALL STICKERS

Football stickers, football stickers cause too much trouble
When you buy more, you end up getting too many doubles,
Last time my teacher took them away,
I pledged to God to make her pay,
Next two weeks I got them back
They were tied in a smelly sack,
I stuck them all in once and for all
No more stickers for me at all.

Joshua Owusu-Afriyie (11)
Wanstead Church Primary School

ANIMAL SEA

The dark waves lapped across the moon,
Swept across the land like a rocket boosting off.
As the sun came down, a golden ray of sunshine passed through me.
Arrows of darkness covered the land with hate and fear.
I, of course, was unaware of this
And the ebony sea grabbed me like a pack of wolves ready to attack!

Freddie Cocker (8)
Wanstead Church Primary School

THE PARK

Swinging, swinging, swinging to and fro,
Over, over, over and low,
Sliding, sliding, sliding up and down,
Bullies, bullies, bullies frown
Shouting, screaming, running all around.
Enjoying, enjoying, enjoying all the sound.

Zoe Aves (11)
Wanstead Church Primary School

WEDNESDAY AFTERNOON

Paint on the tabletops
Paint down my shirt
Paint on the shelves
That dropped down Lizzie's skirt
Brushes on the floor
Paint on the wall
Sink full of soap
How can Ms Smith cope?

Charlotte Hall-Munn (10)
Wanstead Church Primary School

PARENTS

My mum is boring
My dad is snoring

When my mum goes to work
My dad needs a clerk

My mum's cooking is bad
It makes my dad go mad!

Erin Cobby & John Hagon-Torkington (7)
Wanstead Church Primary School

MY BEST FRIEND, MARC

M arc was my best friend.
A lways took me out on his motorbike.
R eally miss him, but will never forget him,
'C ause he is my best friend, Marc.

George Tollady (8)
Whittingham Primary School

WHY?

Why did you leave me?
Why did you go?

Why did you leave me in this world all alone?
I loved it when you kissed me
And told me that you cared.

I loved it when you hugged me
And everything we shared.

I hope you will always be with me
And won't ever go . . .

Because you will always be in my heart
Wherever I may go.

Rachael Clouter (9)
Whittingham Primary School

WHAT IS THE SEA?

The sea is a blue sky
But not that high.

It's a mirror
Out in the open.

It's fluff
With blue stuff.

That's the sea!

Keian Brissett-Martin (10)
Whittingham Primary School

SNOW MAGIC

Snow casting a spell across the Earth
Leaving the planet looking like a snowy, frosty, cold picture
Cars stopping, traffic standing still
This is what happens when snow comes falling down.

Children throwing snowballs, slipping and sliding
Making snowmen with bright orange noses
Elderly staying inside reading the daily news
Eating warm food and drinks so they stay feeling warm
                                             and comfortable
This is what happens when snow comes falling down.

Aeroplanes looking for somewhere to land, causing
                                  the pilot not to see the direction
Helicopters are covered in frost so they can't move
Birds looking for somewhere to land and something to eat
This is what happens when snow comes falling down.

All this happening here and there, comes to a conclusion that
                                            this is called *snow magic!*

Yewande Oloruntade (11)
Whittingham Primary School

SCARED STIFF

Scared stiff,
Can't move,
Miss Evil coming to the door,
A creepy noise from the floor.

Heart thumping,
The door handle moves,
She stands back,
She lifts the latch.

I'm shivering like a mouse,
She's as ugly as a beast,
Green nose,
Sweaty head.

She takes a step forward,
I run,
She steps into the sun,
I say, 'I wish I was at home.'

Emillie Hill (8)
Whittingham Primary School

WHAT ARE THE CLOUDS?

The cloud is a piece of sweet pink candyfloss
waiting patiently to be eaten.

The cloud is like a piece of bubbly foam
floating in paradise.

The cloud is like a waterproof puffer jacket
that makes a gentle rustle.

The cloud is like a drop of strawberry shampoo
that smells like pink blossom.

The cloud is like a spoonful of white mashed potato,
on a white sparkly dinner plate.

The cloud is like a scoop of vanilla ice cream
floating across the sky!

Saniya Ahsan (10)
Whittingham Primary School

My Mum

My mum is the best,
She is kind and caring.

She cheers me up
When I'm feeling down,
She even picks me up,
When I fall down.

My mum is always late
But she is always there for me.

She smells of perfume every day
Gives me sweets as I play.

My mum calls me Sweetie, (or sometimes Sweetie-Pie),
Because I'm nice and sweet, (plus I love pies).

She plays games with me
Even though I lose,
And she always takes the blame for me.

I love her
Just like she loves me.

Naomi Benjamin (9)
Whittingham Primary School

So Loud

It was so loud
I couldn't hear my radio
At full blast!

It was so loud
That I couldn't hear my
Thoughts rustle
Like leaves in a paper bag.

It was so loud
My head started to shake
Like a volcano.

It was so loud
I couldn't hear myself
Thinking!

Yousr Tabir (8)
Whittingham Primary School

SNAKES

Snakes are slippery
Snakes are long
They slither in the jungle
On the branches.
Snakes are slippery
Snakes are long
They slither over you
As long as possible.
Snakes are slippery
Snakes are long
They poison you with fangs
Maybe one or two
Ouch!
Snakes are slippery
Snakes are long
They rattle at you
Snakes are slippery
Snakes are long.

Andrew Christou (8)
Whittingham Primary School

PEACE

I'm in the park all alone
I sit down on the bench
The sky is calm but misty
The birds, I hear their echo

I close my eyes
I'm in a dream
Seeing people smiling
There is no war and no racism either
The world is perfect
And it's also peaceful

I open my eyes
I feel warm
The world is back to its normal self.

I see the sun just peeping behind the cloud
And a huge smile goes across my face.

Zara Marie Ahsan (11)
Whittingham Primary School

SNOW

I'm gliding in the sky,
I'm gliding very high,
I'm going down,
I'm going around now,
I'm on the ground.

Children throwing me around,
Children falling on the ground,
Children like to play with me,
Children's hearts are full of glee.

I make the children cold,
I told you I would be bold,
I make the children laugh,
I make the children act daft!

Michael New (10)
Whittingham Primary School

THE BEAST

The beast of fire with its horns
Came crashing through healing ways
In a fit of pure fury
He burnt me to cinders
And carried on his rampage.

Down and down the whirlpool I went
Till out I came
Reborn and ready to kill.

I travelled for miles and still no sign
Or that fiend that slaughtered me.
I found a sword that I would use to straighten the fiend.

Then a sort of rumbling came from the ground,
I saw the beast straight in front of me,
I stabbed and slashed with my sword.

My eyes were red as fire.

The beast dropped with a ding,
Vanished into thin air,
I had won,
I would live.
Now I would have to look for my family.

Gamal James (10)
Whittingham Primary School

MY BIRTHDAY'S BEEN CANCELLED

I wake up
I see my mum looking sad
She says my birthday's been cancelled
I'm going to be 8 all my life
I get really sad
I have no present
No cake
I go to my room and cry
I can imagine
I am 27
Still in year 4!
Not learning much
Not going to university
No friends, no nothing!

Arnold Kaloki (9)
Whittingham Primary School

WHAT ARE THE STARS?

The star is like flashing thunder,
shining brightly up in the sky.

The star is a golden diamond
floating in the wavy sea.

The star is a glittering seed growing
silently from the sky.

The star is glitter shining above
the sky.

The star is a still candle next to the
burning fire.

Hansah Shafiq (9)
Whittingham Primary School

I Like Winter Very Happily

I like winter very happily.
I like wind very happily.
I like snow very happily.
I like bikes zooming across me.
I like going on trains that go very, very fast.
I like looking at trains that go very, very fast
And zoom across me.
I like people loving other people.
I like the head teacher, who is very, very kind.
Sometimes she is.
I like me which is a little bit naughty.

Alex Du-Gal (8)
Whittingham Primary School

My Waterfall

As my sister and I play in this waterfall,
The sun is so bright and it's in the corner of my eye.

As my sister and I play in this waterfall,
The water is coming down on us.

As my sister and I play in this waterfall,
I love my sister so much.

Rebecca Scott (10)
Whittingham Primary School

Snow

As the snow comes falling down
And finds its way onto the ground

I look out from my window, the snow is flat and white,
It looks just like my fluffy furry blanket that
I sleep with at night.

I pass the tall trees as I'm running by
And sweep the snow nice and dry.

Then I look up into the sky
And see the snowflakes floating by

The snow falls on my hand and drifts into another land.

Zuharia Arshad (10)
Whittingham Primary School

School

I'm the loneliest child in school,
I have no friends at all,
Everyone has friends, I don't!
If I ask someone to play with me, they won't,
I wish I had one friend to play with me,
I'm the loneliest child you see,
I try to play with my sisters, they don't know how to play,
So I just sit on the bench all day.
'I wonder if I'll get a friend?' I say,
If I ever get a friend who's there,
I'll treat her with love and care.

Jordene Battye (9)
Whittingham Primary School

WINTER

Winter comes
Softly drifting down
All around the house
Down the town
Now the air has filled
With winter weather
Snow is falling down
Over rooftop
Over web
Glistening tiny shed
Frosty leaf
Brown and red
On the ground
In the town
Snow comes falling down.

Dionne Cottoy-Rogers (9)
Whittingham Primary School

FRIENDS

Having friends is the best
New friends are special guests
Sticking together,
Working together,
Sharing together,
Friends, friends are the best.

Leah Martin (10)
Whittingham Primary School

IN THE NIGHT

As dark as a cupboard,
As cold as a fridge,
As I tiptoe down the stairs,
Shadows here and shadows there,
Is there a witch somewhere?
Tiptoe, tiptoe, through the hall,
Is that a really ugly ghoul?
It's nearly as spooky as a cave,
Suddenly I see the kitchen door,
But then I creak on the floor,
Mum hears me,
She's out of bed,
I run as fast as I can,
I'm dead!

Millie Carter-Phillips (8)
Whittingham Primary School